Geography
Global Environments and Climatic Regions

TERRA

Prof. Dr. Gregor C. Falk, Elke Storz

Rolf Bächle, Philipp Bürgel, Peter Metschar,
Denise A. Nitsche, Franz-Josef Wallmeier

Ernst Klett Verlag
Stuttgart · Leipzig

How to work with TERRA bilingual

Different colours for special pages:

Warm-up pages (red)
Starting a new topic.

Work pages
On the main pages you can find easy texts and interesting material.

Skill pages (blue)
Important geography skills step by step.

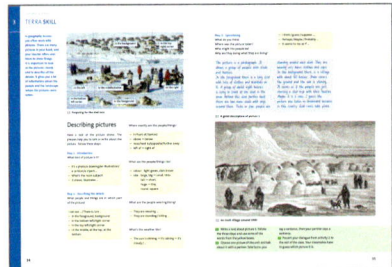

Orientation pages (orange)
Focus on language and put important information from the unit into context

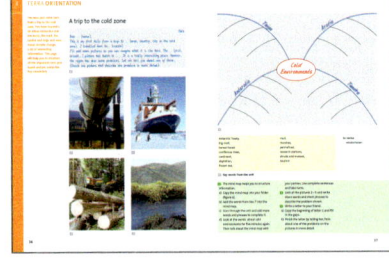

Exercise pages (green)
Practise language, geography and skill tasks and find out what you know.

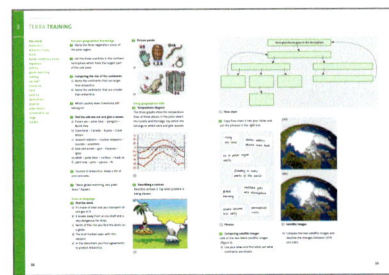

Margin column:

Page 18
Interpreting climate graphs

The red arrow shows the way to another page in your book where you can find extra information.

matchbox
   Streichholzschachtel
running water
   fließend Wasser

You can find important vocabulary at the side of each page and in some pictures.

Appendix:

A
Air pressure: The weight of air pressing down on the Earth's surface.
Antarctica: An area south of the Antarctic Circle. Ice is on most of the

Important words from the book you often need in geography are explained in the appendix.

barometer	15
bauxite	95
biosphere	6f.
black earth	44
Boerde	40, 44

Index: The words in **bold print** are explained in "key words explained".

English	German	Example
A		
absorb	aufnehmen	The carbo
accumulation	Ablagerung	accumula
according to	entsprechend	according

You can look up words in the English – German word list. An example phrase shows you how to use the word in context.

Extra material on the Internet:

🎧 **Listening**
Norilsk – an industrial ‚island' in the Siberian tundra
104510-0306

Online – links show you the way to interesting information on www.klett.de/online.
You can choose between Listening, Surf the net, Extra material and worksheets on the topics..

The online links are always at the top of each page. Just put the online – link in the search machine and you will find material on your topic.

Content

1

Global environments and climatic regions   4

The earth – system and spheres   6
The water cycle   8

2

Atmosphere and world climate   10

Atmosphere and solar radiation   12
Weather and climate   14
The seasons   16
Interpreting climate graphs   18

3

Cold environments   20

Polar regions: Arctic and Antarctica   22
Antarctica in danger   24
The Inuit – Life in snow and ice   26
Will the polar bears die out?   28
Tundra – the empty land   30
Taiga – the snowy forest   32
Describing pictures   34
A trip to the cold zone   36
Training   38

4

Temperate and subtropical zones   40

Cold in the north, warm in the south, wet in the west and dry in the east   42
Gone with the wind …   44
Living on the sunny side   46
Hotter, drier, wetter and more extreme – Climate change in Europe?   48
How to analyse charts   50

5

Hot desert – Dry climates   52

Desert types   54
Life in the desert   56
Nomadic life – Joining the Tuareg   58
Green islands in the desert – Oases   60
How to present   62
Focus on deserts   64
Training   66

6

Sahel, the fringe – Savanna   68

Rainy and dry seasons in savannas   70
Different types of savannas   72
Farming in the Sahel   74
Desertification   76
Lake Chad – a disappearing livelihood?   78
Dry areas in the world   80
Discussion: Fishbowl   82

7

Very wet and very hot   84

Making holidays in a tropical resort   86
A dense, green and tall forest   88
Food chain and endangered species   90
Rain, rain, rain   92
Living in harmony with nature: the Yanomami   94
Destroying or saving our "green lung"?   96
Air pressure and winds in January and July   98
Working with thematic maps   100
Training   102

Key:
TERRA **SKILL**
TERRA **ORIENTATION**
TERRA **TRAINING**

1 Global environments and climatic regions

An astronaut in space sees our planet as a small blue ball in the universe. This picture changes when he gets closer to the Earth: there are many different environments around the globe like deserts or rainforests. In this book you will learn about natural environments and how people's activities influence systems on Earth: global systems.

1 A glacier
2 Taiga in Siberia
3 An oasis town in a desert
4 Tropical rainforest

2

3

4

Global environments and climatic regions

1 Our eight planets without Pluto

The earth – systems and spheres

to survive	überleben
to develop	sich entwickeln
to rotate	umkreisen
to spin	drehen
on their own axis	um ihre eigene Achse
geosphere	Geosphäre
due to	auf Grund
gravity	Schwerkraft
scientist	Wissenschaftler
boundary	Grenze
liquid	Flüssigkeit
dust	Staub

The third planet from the sun is our home. It is the only planet we know where life can survive. Life has developed over millions of years. All planets rotate around the sun and spin on their own axis at different speeds. One Jupiter year for example is more than 11 years on earth. A day on Jupiter takes only 10 hours.

There is not much material in space, as it is a vacuum. The temperature in space is about −270 °C.

The earth is a closed system. That means no material is lost into space and no material comes in. Only energy can come in and go out. This system is called **geosphere** (see figure 3).

Poor Pluto, it is not a planet any more. In 2006 the International Astronomic Union said what a planet is:

A planet
– needs to go around the Sun
– is large enough to have become round due to its own gravity

And that is what Pluto did not do – it is simply too small.

2 Definition of a planet

Spheres within the geosphere

There are smaller systems which are part of the geosphere. Scientists say that our blue planet has four main spheres: the **lithosphere**, the **atmosphere**, the **biosphere**, and the **hydrosphere**. There are no boundaries between them. They are open systems. Material, gases and liquids can move between them. For example, water can be found high in the atmosphere as clouds, and then moves through the lithosphere as rain. A volcano can throw dust from the lithosphere high up into the atmosphere.

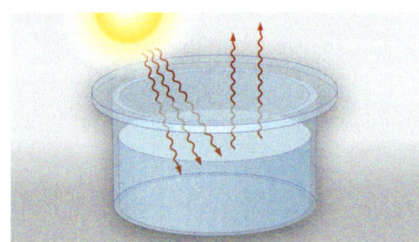

3 Geosphere, a closed system in space

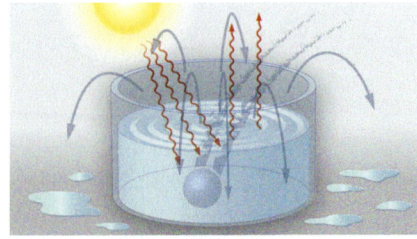

4 All spheres in the geosphere are open

5 Four spheres in one picture

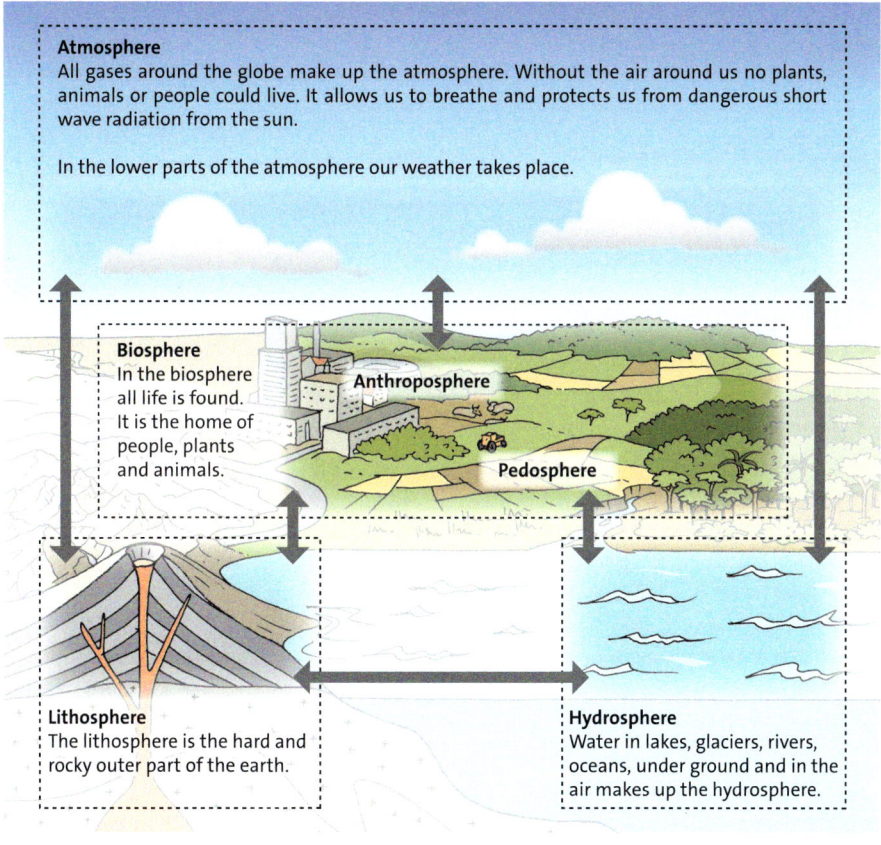

Atmosphere
All gases around the globe make up the atmosphere. Without the air around us no plants, animals or people could live. It allows us to breathe and protects us from dangerous short wave radiation from the sun.

In the lower parts of the atmosphere our weather takes place.

Biosphere
In the biosphere all life is found. It is the home of people, plants and animals.

Anthroposphere

Pedosphere

Lithosphere
The lithosphere is the hard and rocky outer part of the earth.

Hydrosphere
Water in lakes, glaciers, rivers, oceans, under ground and in the air makes up the hydrosphere.

6 The geosphere and its spheres

lithosphere
  Lithosphäre
atmosphere
  Atmosphäre
biosphere
  Biosphäre
hydrosphere
  Hydrosphäre
short wave radiation
  kurzwellige Strahlung
to boil
  kochen
glacier
  Gletscher

1 Picture 5 shows the four spheres. Describe each of them in your own words.

2 Look up more facts about Jupiter (size, distance from sun etc.). Make a table and compare it to the Earth (Internet).

3 Discuss if the following systems are open or closed systems: microwave, pot with boiling water, inside of an airplane, oven.

Global environments and climatic regions

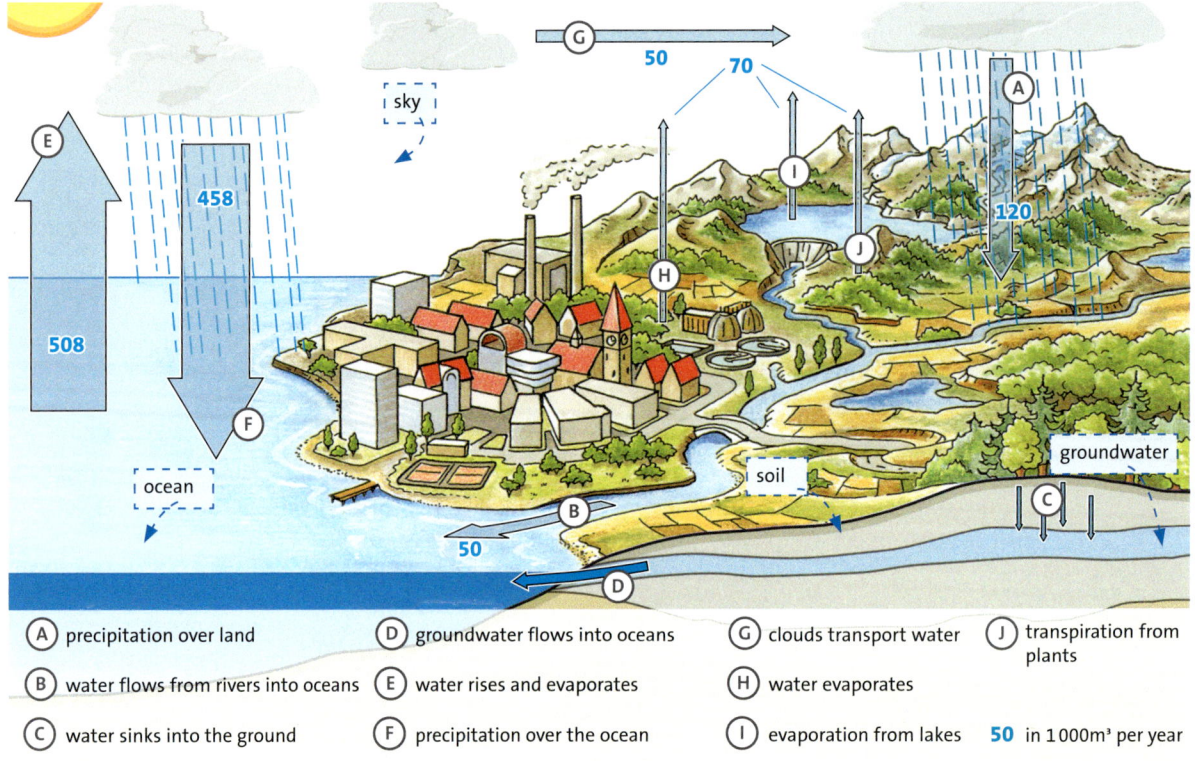

- (A) precipitation over land
- (B) water flows from rivers into oceans
- (C) water sinks into the ground
- (D) groundwater flows into oceans
- (E) water rises and evaporates
- (F) precipitation over the ocean
- (G) clouds transport water
- (H) water evaporates
- (I) evaporation from lakes
- (J) transpiration from plants
- 50 in 1 000m³ per year

1 The water cycle

water cycle
  Wasserkreislauf
water vapour
  Wasserdampf
evaporation
  Verdunstung
transpiration
  Verdunstung
sweat
  Schweiß
to condense
  kondensieren
liquid
  Flüssigkeit
droplet
  Tröpfchen
economic
  wirtschaftlich
shortage
  Knappheit
drought
  Dürre
surplus
  Überschuss

The water cycle

Nothing is lost in the geosphere. Material only moves from one place to another. One example is the **water cycle**. The sun heats up the water on earth. Water vapour rises from the warm ground into the atmosphere (see figure 1: E, H, I). When water changes from liquid to gas it is called **evaporation**.
Another way water can go back into the air is **transpiration**. Plants for example take water in from the ground and then let it out through their leaves (J). Transpiration helps plants to stay cool. People and animals can do something similar, they keep cool when it's hot by sweating. The sweat then evaporates from their skin.
The higher up in the sky the cooler the air becomes. That is why water vapour starts to **condense**, that means water changes from a gas to a liquid forming small droplets. The clouds we can see are billions of little water droplets or frozen ice crystals. If the air rises higher, more water vapour condenses and the droplets or crystals get bigger. When they become too large, they fall to the ground (A) or onto the oceans (F) as rain. Rivers and lakes collect some water (I, B) but most of it sinks down through the soil to form the groundwater (C).

There isn't enough water
In many regions around the world people do not have enough fresh water. The problem is that more and more water is needed for more and more people and economic activities. Most of the water is used for agriculture or to produce things in factories. In some countries people take so much water out of the ground that there is almost no groundwater left. Because people use so much water, there are many problems around the world like water shortages and **droughts**.

Extra material
Evaporation and condensation
104510-0101

2 Water is used for everything

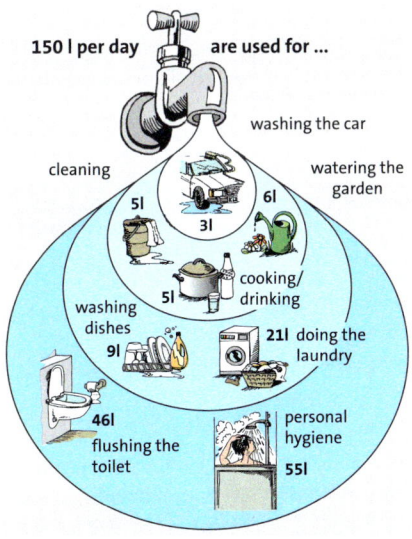

3 150 l per person per day

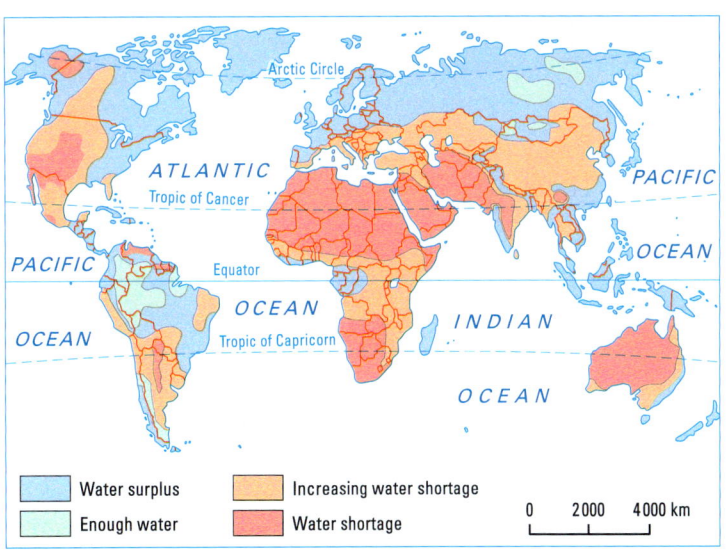

4 How much water is there around the world

1 Describe the water cycle (fig. 1) in your own words. Use these words to help you: to heat up – to turn into vapour – to lose water – to get cold – to change back into liquid

2 Describe the different ways people use water (figures 2 and 3).

3 Water is limited around the world. Name five countries with water shortage and with water surplus (figure 4).

2 Atmosphere and world climate

Take a deep breath and you breathe in a part of our atmosphere. Without the atmosphere life on earth would not be possible. It protects plants animals and people from dangerous short wave radiation.
The natural greenhouse effect keeps our globe warm. If the earth had no atmosphere it would be much colder.

Atmosphere and world climate

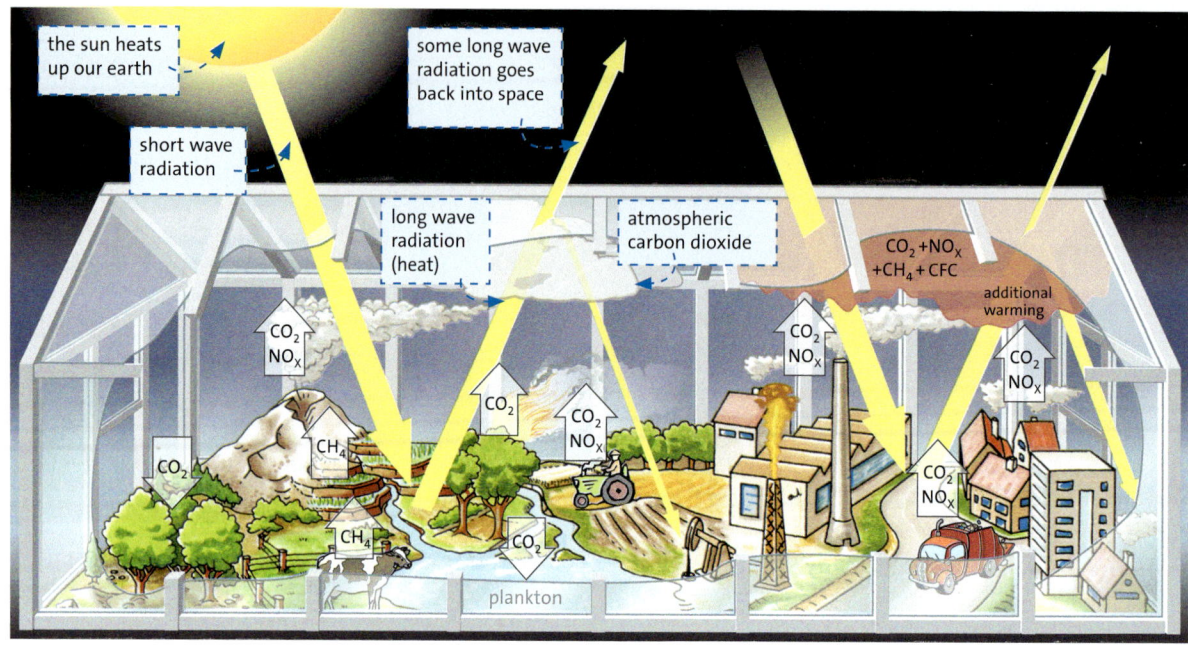

1 Natural and man-made greenhouse effect

Atmosphere and solar radiation

CFC
  FCKW
solar radiation
  Sonneneinstrahlung
layer
  Schicht
ozone layer
  Ozonschicht
air pressure
  Luftdruck
greenhouse
  Treibhaus
sunray
  Sonnenstrahl
short/long wave radiation
  kurzwellige / langwellige Strahlung
to sweat
  schwitzen
to reflect
  zurückstrahlen
to absorb
  aufnehmen, absorbieren
natural/man-made greenhouse effect
  natürlicher / menschgemachter Treibhauseffekt

What is the atmosphere?

The **atmosphere** is a thin layer of gases around the earth (see figure 4). These gases are important because they make the earth warmer (about 15°C), without these gases the temperature would only be -18°C.

The earth's atmosphere is about 480 km and has different layers: the troposphere is where all the weather takes place and where we live. The stratosphere with the **ozone layer**. The mesosphere and the thermosphere (see figure 3).

Air pressure

The **air pressure** outside a plane is a lot less than the air pressure on the ground. There is no exact place where the atmosphere ends, it just gets thinner and thinner.

The unit to describe the air pressure per m² is hPa which stands for Hectopascal. You can often see hPa on weather maps. They are important for meterologists who tell us what the weather will be like in the next few days.

Way of the incoming sunlight

The way of the incoming sunlight can be compared to a greenhouse. Have you ever been in one? It is really hot in there. That's because the sunlight goes through the glass of the greenhouse and the sunrays cannot get out. It gets warmer and warmer inside and the plants can grow a lot faster.

Have a look at figure 1 it shows the way of the incoming sunlight on earth. The sun sends off sunrays (**short wave radiation**). They move through the atmosphere and change into **long wave radiation** (heat) when they reach the ground. Your body is the same in the sun on a hot summer day. Your skin is hit by sunlight and you start to feel warm and sweat.

When the sunrays reach the ground the radiation is reflected and some long wave radiation goes back into space while other is absorbed by the **carbon dioxide** in the atmosphere and warms up the earth. This is called the **natural greenhouse effect**. People also talk about the **man-made greenhouse effect**. What do you know about it?

Air pressure experiment

What you need:
a glass of water, a cardboard sheet

What to do:
1. Fill a glass with water and cover it with a cardboard sheet.
2. Turn the glass upside down, but do not forget to press the cardboard to the glass while turning it!
3. When the glass is upside down, take your hand away.

Results:
What happens?
Try to explain!

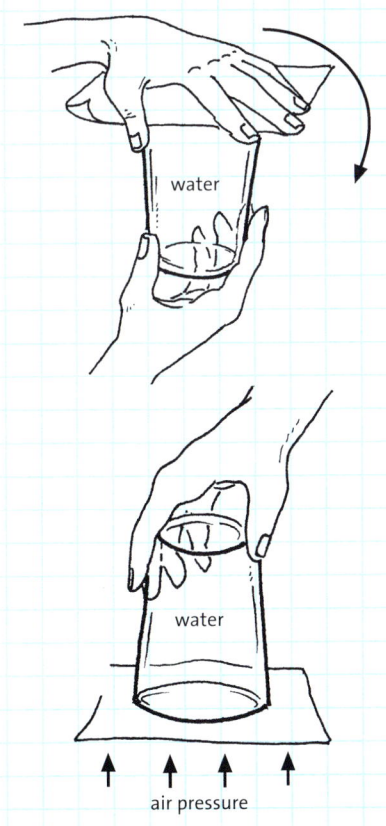

2 Air pressure experiment

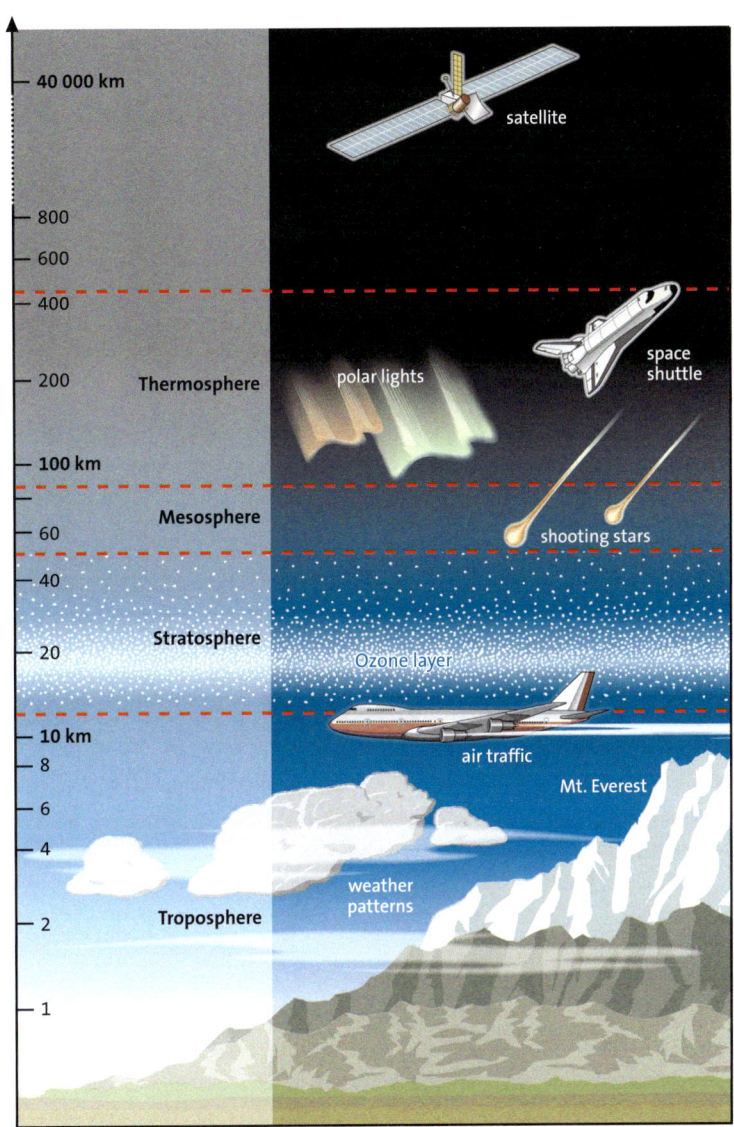

3 Layers of the atmosphere

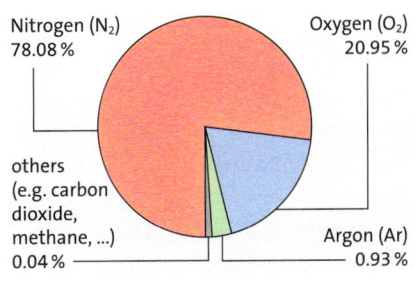

4 Gases in the atmosphere

nitrogen
  Stickstoff
fossil fuels
  fossile Brennstoffe

- - ->
Pages 50/51
How to analyse charts

1 Explain the natural greenhouse effect in your own words.

2 Discuss in which way the burning of fossil fuels from cars or factories may change the temperatures on earth.

13

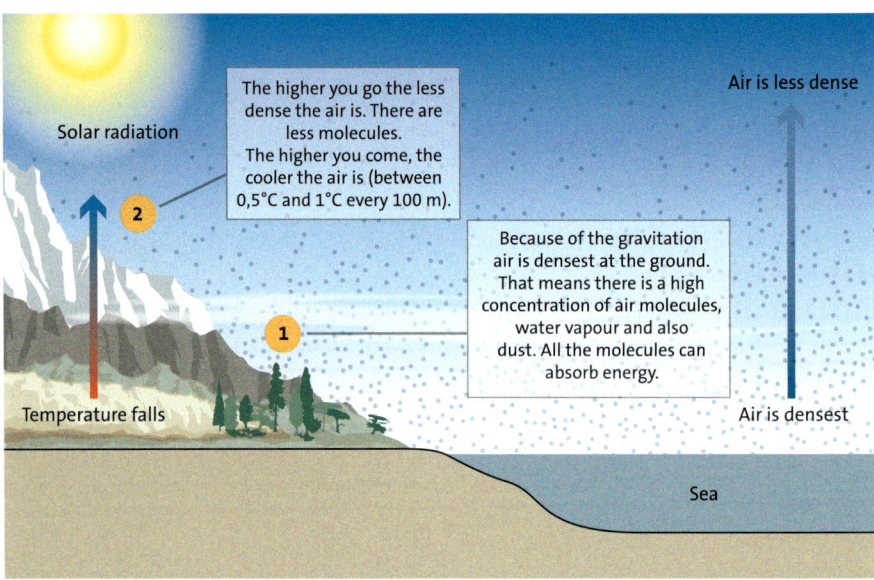

1 Solar radiation and air pressure

Weather and climate

gravitation	
Erdanziehung	
water vapour	
Wasserdampf	
to expect	
erwarten	
to absorb	
aufnehmen	
precipitation	
Niederschlag	
humidity	
Feuchtigkeit	
climate	
Klima	
state	
Zustand	
average	
durchschnittlich	
to replace	
ersetzen	
droplet	
Tröpfchen	

"Climate is what we expect, weather is what we get."
Mark Twain

2

Look out of the window and you can see what the weather is like. You can find out the temperature, how strong the wind is, if it's dry or raining. Weather takes place in the lower parts of the **atmosphere** (troposphere). Temperature, **precipitation**, humidity, clouds, air pressure and wind are elements of the atmosphere that we use to describe the weather at some place. **Weather** is the state of the atmosphere at any given time.

When meteorologists talk about the climate of a place or region they use weather data which they took for a long time (at least 30 years). So **climate** is the average weather in a place. It's what the weather is usually like.

Temperature
The temperature tells us how fast air molecules move. The faster they move, the more energy they hold. When they move fast a thermometer shows high temperatures. Slow moving molecules mean cooler temperatures.

Wind
The earth's warms up differently. In warmer places the air rises, then cooler air moves in to replace the warmer air. In cooler regions the cold air sinks to the ground. Wind is a large mass of moving air molecules.

Rain
Warm air rises and becomes colder. The cooler the air is the less water vapour can it keep. Droplets begin to form. When the droplets are too large they fall to the earth as rain.

3 Weather elements

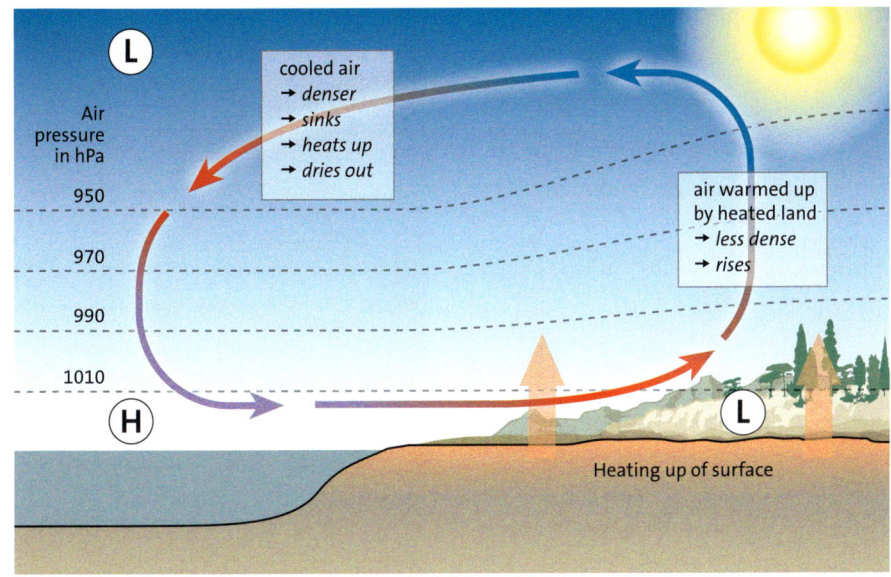

4 The land - sea wind system at daytime

device
Gerät

5 Equipment you need to measure the weather

1 Explain the difference between weather and climate.

2 Look at box 5. It shows equipment you need to measure the weather.
a) Find the name of each device from the boxes. Then add the German word.
b) What do you think they measure?

3 Figure 4 shows the land–sea wind system at daytime. Work with a partner.

a) Explain it with the help of figure 4. Tip: Wind always blows from H to L.
b) Now think about the situation at night. Draw a a diagram to show the system at night. Explain! Tip: It needs more time for water to heat up during day but it can keep the heat better at night than the land.

Atmosphere and world climate

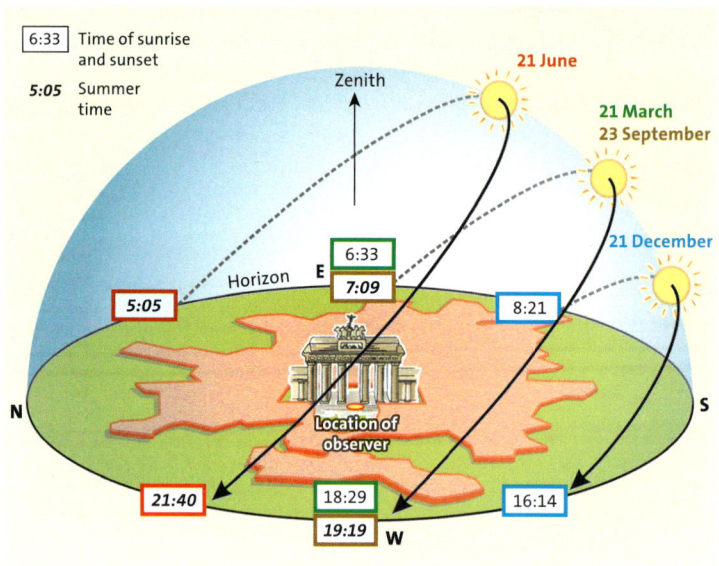

1 Position of the Sun at different times of the year in Germany

The seasons

The year has **seasons**. Countries like Germany which are quite far from the **equator** have up to four seasons: spring, summer, autumn and winter. In these regions it is warmer in summer and colder in winter.

Closer to the equator you will find only two seasons: a **dry season** and a **rainy season**. Around the equator it is hot and humid all year round. There are no seasons at all.

Some simple facts explain the seasons
1. In one year (365 days) the earth rotates around the sun.
2. The axis of the earth is tilted at 23.5 degrees.

This means during our summer the **northern hemisphere** is tilted towards the sun. This means there is more energy, it is warm. At the same time it is a lot colder in the **southern hemisphere** because it is tilted away from the sun (see figures 5 and 6). In our winter it is the other way around. During one year the position of the sun moves between 23.26° north (**Tropic of Cancer**) and 23.26° south (**Tropic of Capricorn**) of the equator.

zenith
  Zenit; Senkrechtstand der Sonne
seasons
  Jahreszeiten
equator
  Äquator
dry season
  Trockenzeit
rainy season
  Regenzeit
humid
  feucht
to rotate
  rotieren, umkreisen
tilted
  geneigt
angle
  Winkel
latitude
  Breitengrad
hemisphere
  Hemisphäre, Halbkugel
Tropic of Capricorn
  südlicher Wendekreis
Tropic of Cancer
  nördlicher Wendekreis

2 A tree in four seasons

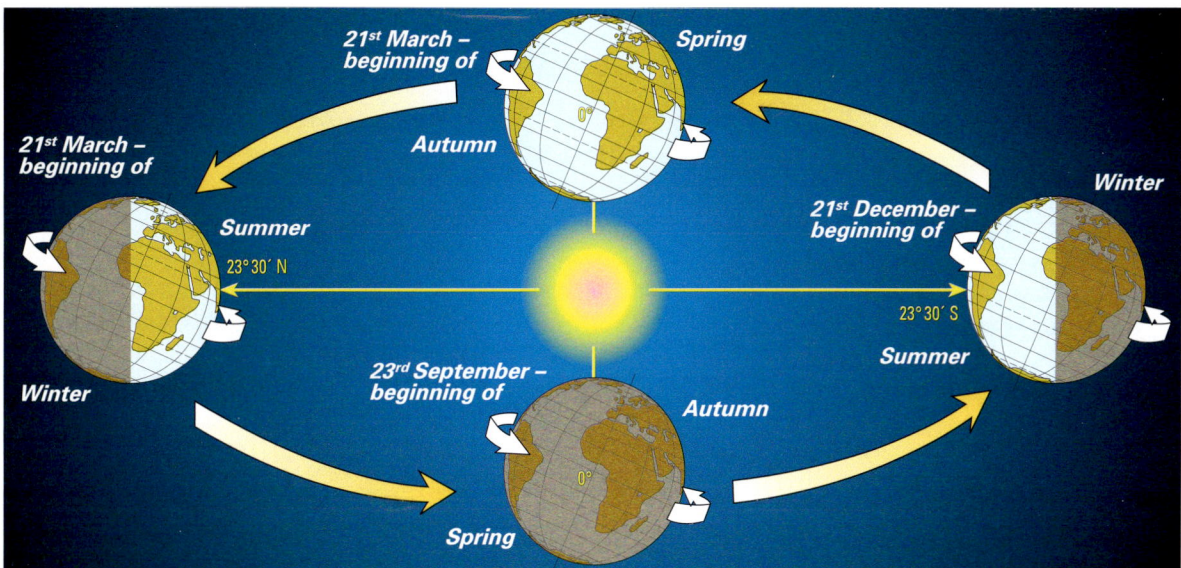

3 The earth rotates around the sun

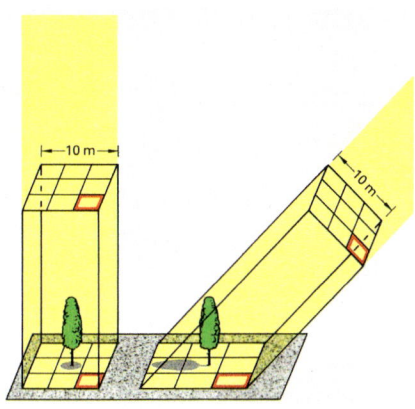

4 A straight angle heats up the earth more than a flat angle

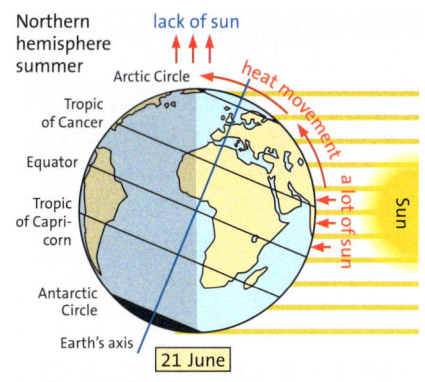

5 Summer in the northern and winter in the southern hemisphere

6 Palm tree in the sun

surface
  Oberfläche
lack of
  Mangel an

1 Figure 5 shows the summer situation in the northern hemisphere. Draw a diagram to show the situation in winter.

2 Find out which climatic regions are between the Tropic of Cancer and the Tropic of Capricorn (atlas).

3 Photo 6 shows a palm tree in the sun.
a) At which angle was the sun when the picture was taken?
b) Locate the place of the photo on fig. 5.

4 Explain why there are different seasons. Use your own words.
Phrases to help you:
– the earth is tilted on its axis.
– directly over the equator
– the earth rotates around the sun
– at the beginning of spring / summer / …

4 "The effect of the solar radiation depends on latitude." Explain this statement.

TERRA SKILL

Climate graphs show the climate of a specific place. You can use them to find out the average temperature and precipitation of different months during the year. You need climate graphs when you want to know what the climate is like at a place you don't know for example, this may be useful when you want to go on holiday.

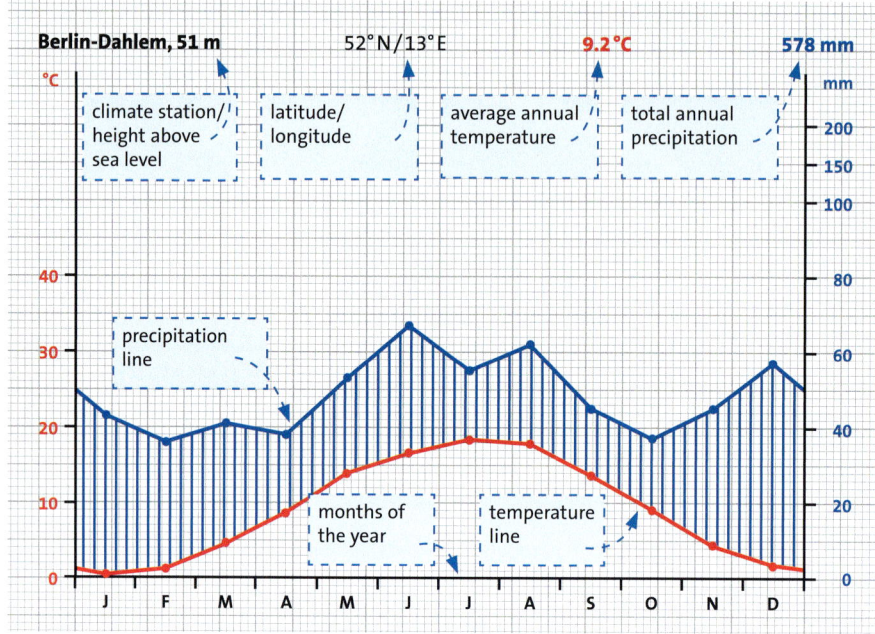

1 Climate graph of Berlin-Dahlem

Interpreting climate graphs

Step 1: Position
Find out the position of the station (atlas).

- The height of the station is ____ m above sea level.
- It is in/near _____.

Step 2: Precipitation and temperature
Read off the annual average temperature and precipitation.
Then find out which is the warmest and the coldest as well as the wettest and driest month.

- The annual average temperature/precipitation over the year is ____.
- The warmest/coldest month with ____°C on average is ____.
- The wettest/driest month with ____ mm precipitation is ____.

Describe the changes during the year (temperature, precipitation and aridity/humidity).

- With ____°C the temperature range is low/high.
- The temperature line has one/two maxima.
- The month with the highest amount of precipitation is ____.
- From ____ till ____ the ____ line is below/above the ____ line.
- There are ____ arid and ____ humid months.

Step 3: Give reasons
Name reasons for climate of the city and, with the help of an atlas, try to find out in which climate zone the station could be.

- One reason for the climate is _____.
- The place/city belongs to the _____.

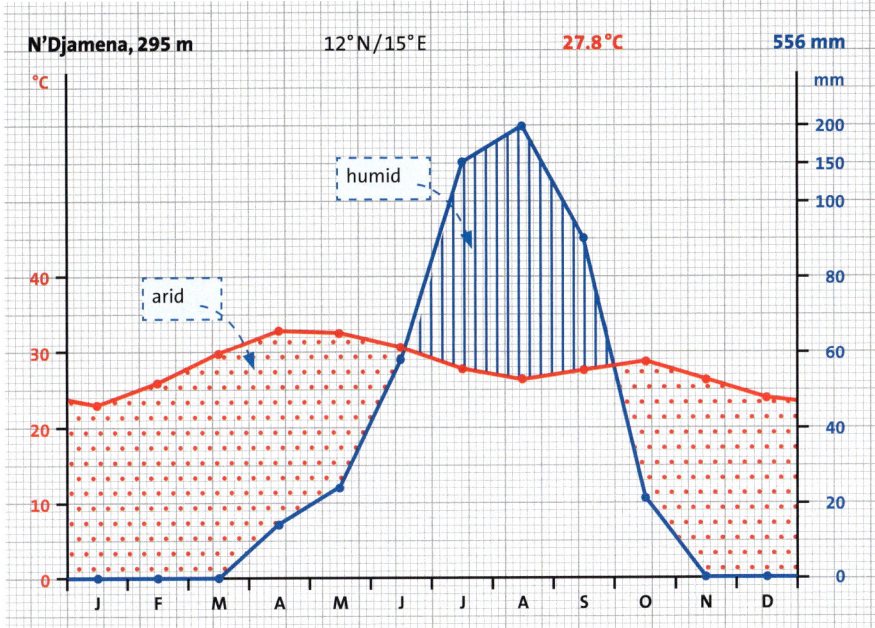

2 Climate graph of N'Djamena

Berlin is a city in Germany. The height of the station is 51 m above sea level and its coordinates are 52°N and 13°E. The average temperature over the year is 9,2 °C. The total precipitation is 587 mm. The warmest month is August and the coldest months are January and February. The driest months are February and October and most rain falls in July. There is no dry or wet season. Precipitation falls throughout the whole year. There is an increase in temperature from the winter months to the summer months. Berlin belongs to the temperate climate zone with cold winters and relatively warm summers. The climate is like this because Berlin is not close to the sea but located more in the middle of the continent. The climate is called semi-continental.

3 Describing the climate graph of Berlin

average
 durchschnittlich
annual
 jährlich
precipitation
 Niederschlag
height above sea level
 Höhe über dem Meeresspiegel
aridity
 Aridität, Trockenheit
humidity
 Humidität, Feuchtigkeit
temperature range
 Temperaturbereich
amount
 Menge
semi-continental
 Übergangsklima

1 Compare the climate of Berlin with that of N'Djamena. What differences do you notice (humidity, temperature, etc.)?

2 Interpret the climate graph of N'Djamena with the help of the three steps.

3 Work in small groups and find out how you can tell whether a climate graph is of a place in the northern or southern hemisphere.

19

3 Cold environments

"This is my hometown Ilussiat. It's on the west coast of Greenland. I live in one of the houses on the hill. The red building in the front is my school. It's very cold up in the north, but we have a lot of fun in the snow and on the ice. We build igloos, play football and ice hockey".

Fririk

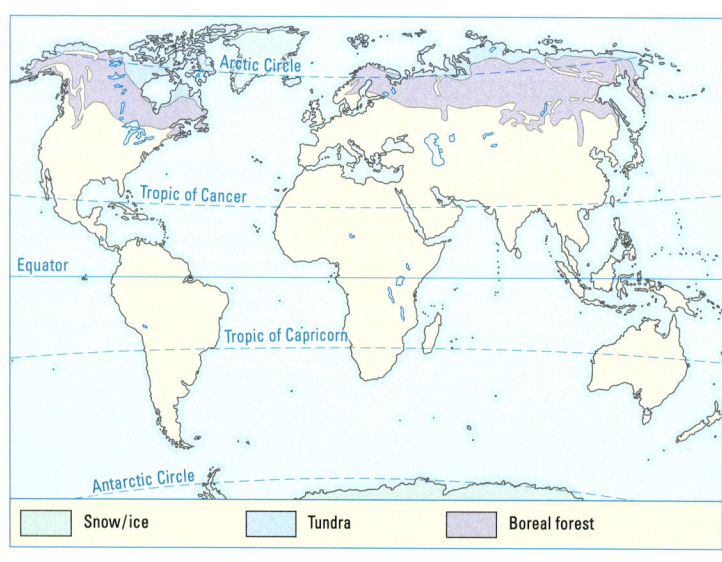

1

2 Fririk's hometown Ilussiat

Cold environments

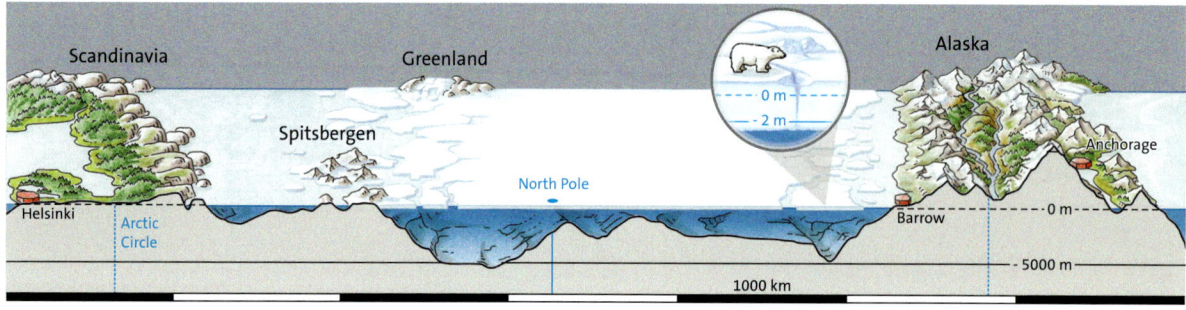

1 West-east cross section through the Arctic

Polar regions: Arctic and Antarctica

polar region
  Polargebiet
North Pole
  Nordpol
South Pole
  Südpol
Arctic
  Arktis
Arctic Circle
  Polarkreis
Antarctic Circle
  südlicher Polarkreis
Antarctica
  Antarktis
to surround
  umgeben
particular
  bestimmten
research station
  Forschungsstation
surface
  Oberfläche

← - -
Page 18
Interpreting climate graphs

The areas around the North and South Pole are called **polar regions**. Blue and white are the colours which dominate the landscape there: blue because of the water and the sky, white because of ice and snow. But there are also a lot of differences between the area around the **North Pole** and the area around the **South Pole**.

Arctic
When we travel north of the **Arctic Circle** we get to the **Arctic**. In the middle of the Arctic we find a large frozen sea. Around this sea there are three continents.

Antarctica
On the opposite side of the world, south of the **Antarctic Circle**, there is a continent with high mountains which is called **Antarctica**. Ice covers most of this continent. Three oceans surround Antarctica. It does not belong to a particular country. But many countries have research stations there.

- On top of the land there are **ice sheets**. These are thick masses of **glacier** ice. We mainly find them in Greenland and on Antarctica.
- A special form of ice are the **ice shelves**. You can find them at the edge of the Antarctic. The top is formed by frozen precipitation, the base by frozen seawater.
- **Drift ice** are pieces of ice that float on the surface of the water. Sometimes the wind and water push drift ice together so that it is hard for ships to go through it. This is called **pack ice**.
- Icebergs are very dangerous for ships. They break away from ice shelves or ice sheets and float in the open water. They can travel thousands of kilometres. You can only see a small part of an iceberg, because most of it is underwater.

3 There are four different kinds of ice in these cold regions

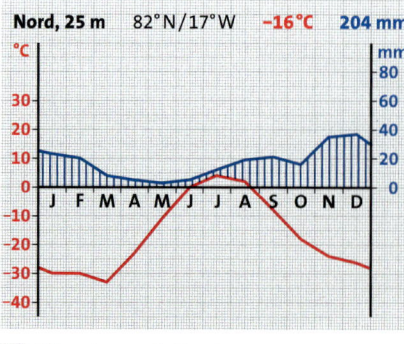

2 Climate graph Nord

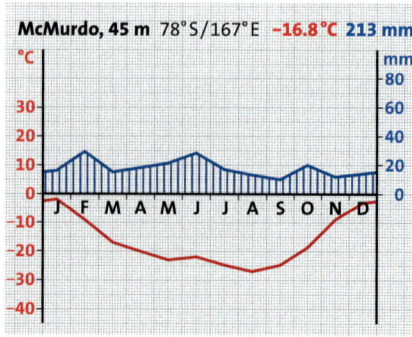

4 Climate graph Mc Murdo

Worksheet

The race to the South Pole
104510-0301

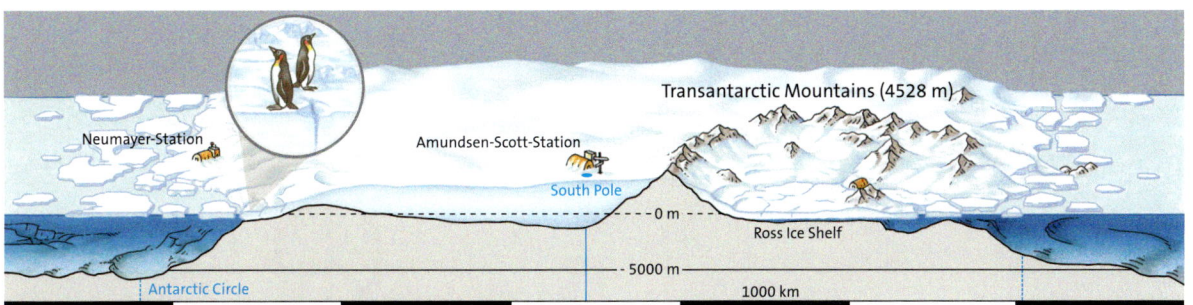

5 West-east cross section through Antarctica

6

8

7

9

ice sheet
  Inlandeis
glacier
  Gletscher
ice shelf
  Schelfeis
edge
  Rand
precipitation
  Niederschlag
drift ice
  Treibeis
surface
  Oberfläche
pack ice
  Packeis
to float
  treiben
explorers
  Forscher

1 Look at the pages about the Arctic and Antarctica in your atlas.
a) Name the three continents which surround the Arctic Ocean and the three oceans which surround Antarctica.
b) Find out how far you must travel to cross the Arctic Ocean from Scandinavia (North Cape) to Alaska (Cape Barrow).

2 Compare the two climate graphs. Describe differences and similarities (climate graphs 2 and 4, atlas).

3 Read the text about the different kinds of ice (text 3). Match the pictures 6 – 9 with the right description.

4 Explorers and adventurers
a) Look at the figures 1 and 5. Discuss: Was it harder for explorers to get to the North Pole or to the South Pole? Why?
b) Find out who was the first man on the North Pole and the first man on the South Pole.

23

Cold environments

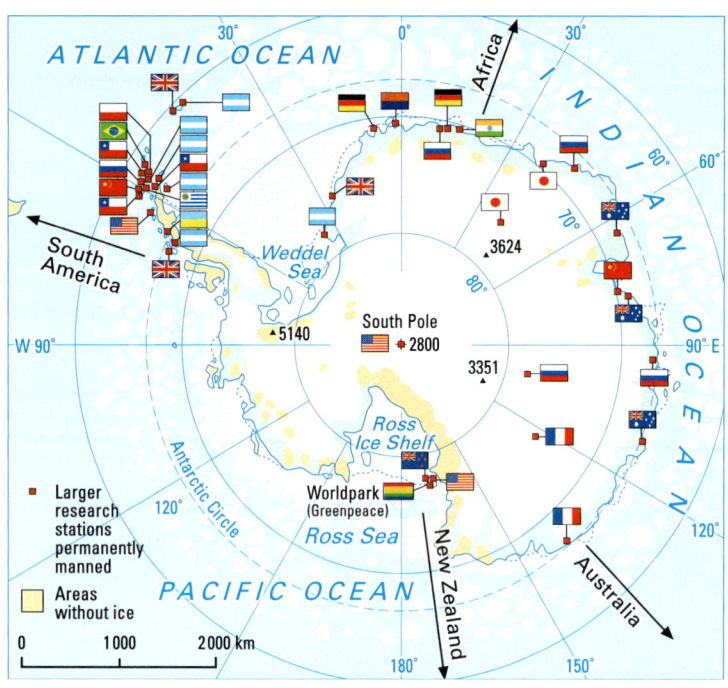

1 Important research stations in Antarctica

Antarctica in danger

permanently
  ständig, dauerhaft
to be manned
  besetzt sein
scientist
  Wissenschaftler
to divide
  teilen
research station
  Forschungsstation
treaty
  Vertrag
to claim
  beanspruchen
raw materials
  Rohstoffe
nuclear weapon
  Atomwaffe
to disturb
  stören
rubbish
  Müll
to pollute
  verschmutzen

Did you know: Only four babies were ever born in Antarctica. The people who live in Antarctica are all scientists. They only stay on the continent for a few months. In summer there are about 5,000 scientists, in winter only about 1,000.

Antarctica does not belong to one country. It is divided into different parts. Fifteen countries have their research stations in Antarctica. Germany also has one area: the German research station is called Georg-Neumayer-Station.

Is tourism bad for Antarctica?

Antarctica is a very interesting place. That is why more and more tourists visit Antarctica each year. Ten years ago there were only 7,500 visitors per year, in 2008/09 more than 30,000 people came to the white continent. In the next few years people believe that there will be even more tourists.

2 The Antarctic Treaty

Scientists are not very happy that Antarctica has become so popular for tourists. They say that the ships and the people disturb the animals at sea and on land. Some birds are already in danger of dying out. The visitors also leave rubbish there and pollute the environment.

 **Surf the net**
Webcam Neumayer Station
104510-0302

 **Listening**
A trip to Antarctica
104510-0303

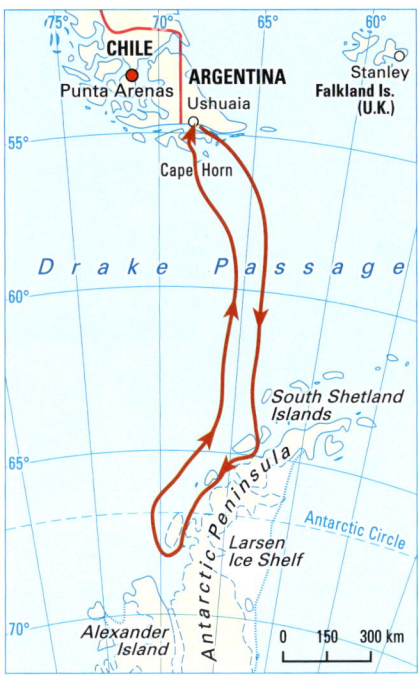

3 A trip to Antarctica

5 Tourists having lunch in Antarctica

4 Who gets the best picture?

Peninsula
Halbinsel

Page 38
Exercise 6

1 List the countries which have research stations in Antarctica (map 1, Internet).
2 The Antarctic Treaty is very important.
a) Name reasons for the Antarctic treaty.
b) Decide which of the five points is the most important one and say why.
3 Imagine you are the penguin in picture 4. Describe your feelings. These words can help you: It is possible that … / I think … / I suppose… / I imagine… / maybe / perhaps.

4 Listen to the text about the trip to Antarctica.
a) Name the activities that tourists can do on Antarctica.
b) Explain why you would like or not like to do this.
5 Figure out how long the journey of the "Polar Star" is in kilometres (atlas).
6 Create a leaflet for tourists on Antarctica in which you tell them what they can do and what they cannot do.

Cold environments

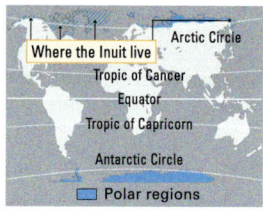

2 An Inuit village in 1904

The Inuit – life in snow and ice

Inuit
 Inuit
agriculture
 Landwirtschaft
to hunt
 jagen
nomad
 Nomade

In the past …
For thousands of years the **Inuit** have been living in areas around the Arctic Ocean. Agriculture is not possible there because it is too cold. In the past the Inuit only ate meat from the animals which they hunted. The most important animal for them was the seal which gave them everything they needed to survive.

The Inuit didn't only stay at one place. They moved around to follow the animals; they were **nomads**. On land they used dog sleds to transport things, on the water they travelled with kayaks.

3 Seals are very important for the Inuit

4 An Inuit hunting in a kayak

Surf the net
A day in the life of an Inuit child
104510-0304

Listening
The Canadian Inuit
104510-0305

5

7

6

8

... and today

Not many of the 100,000 Inuit who live today remember the life of their grandparents. Their life is completely different. They live in small coloured wooden houses called "matchboxes" with running water and electricity. They buy the things for their daily life in supermarkets and have motor vehicles to travel or transport things. For most of them hunting is only a leisure activity.

Inuit children like playing football or basketball. They wear modern clothes like jeans and baseball caps. At school they learn English. This helps them to understand the TV programmes they watch and the computer programmes they use; but they also need English to find a job when they are older. There are not many jobs in their villages. So they must leave their homes to look for a job in the next larger town.

matchbox
   Streichholzschachtel
running water
   fließend Wasser
electricity
   Strom
vehicle
   Fahrzeug
leisure activity
   Freizeitbeschäftigung

---

1 Use map 1 and the atlas. Name the countries where Inuit live today.
2 Look at drawing 2 from 1904 and list ideas on how the Inuit lived a hundred years ago.
3 Find out which things in picture 2 the Inuit made from seals.
4 Write down captions for each of the pictures 5–8. Then talk about the pictures with a partner.

5 Read the texts about the life of the Inuit on pages 26, 27. Draw a table and compare the life in the past and today.

	in the past	today
food	from animals	from animals and from the supermarket
learning	...	
...		

27

Cold environments

[1] Global warming T-shirt

← - -
Page 12
Natural greenhouse effect

[2] The polar bear is in danger

Will the polar bears die out?

cause
  Grund
effect
  Auswirkung
greenhouse gas
  Treibhausgas
carbon dioxide
  Kohlendioxid
methane
  Methan
long wave radiation
  langwellige Strahlung
global warming
  globale Erwärmung
scientist
  Wissenschaftler
to disappear
  verschwinden

Causes and effects of global warming
In the atmosphere there are **greenhouse gases** like **carbon dioxide** and **methane**. These gases are important because they throw some of the **long wave radiation** back to the earth and make the earth warmer. Without these gases the earth would be much colder (see page 12).
But today we put more and more greenhouse gases into the atmosphere. The earth is getting warmer and warmer. This process is called "**global warming**."

In the Arctic this warming has dramatic effects because the Arctic is warming faster than the rest of the world. Scientists say that by 2015 the Arctic will be ice-free in summer. This will effect not only people and animals that live there, but also the rest of the world. The polar bear is a symbol for all animals in the cold zone. It needs the pack ice to travel and to catch seals. They are its most important food. In ten years the Arctic will lose about 9% of its ice, so it will be more difficult for polar bears to find food. A professor from Canada said, "When the sea ice disappears, the polar bears will disappear, too." It is possible that in 50 years we can only see polar bears in our zoos.

3 Rising temperature in the Arctic?

The big melt

"The big melt has begun," a scientist said. There are not only consequences for the people and animals that live in the Arctic region. There are four negative effects on the whole world: when more and more ice melts the sea level will rise. That means a lot of low lying areas close to the coast can be flooded.

The ice caps of the Arctic are fresh water. When they melt they will make the oceans less salty. That will change the sea currents in the oceans. That means that the climate of the whole world will also change.

Ice is white and reflects the sunlight back into space. If the ice melts, the darker surface will absorb more sunlight. That means the earth is again getting warmer.

The warmer temperatures will melt a lot of permafrost. The micro-organisms in the ground will produce more methane. **Methane** is a greenhouse gas and when more of it gets into the atmosphere global warming becomes worse.

1 Give reasons why polar bears are finding it harder to survive as the Arctic warms up.
2 Describe the man-made greenhouse effect in your own words (text, page 12).
3 List key words for the negative effects of the big melt on the whole world.

4 The Arctic ice is melting

4 Compare the two maps about the Arctic ice (map 4) and figure out how much of the Arctic ice has disappeared since 1980 (in per cent).
5 Look at the T-shirt on page 28. Would you wear this T-shirt? Give reasons for your choice.
6 Make a list of the activities that can help to stop global warming.

consequences
    Auswirkungen
sea level
    Meeresspiegel
to be flooded
    überflutet sein
ice caps
    Eisschicht/-kappe
fresh water
    Süßwasser
sea current
    Meeresströmung
to reflect
    zurückstrahlen
to absorb
    absorbieren, aufnehmen
permafrost
    Dauerfrostboden

Pages 38/39
Exercises 7, 11–13

Cold environments

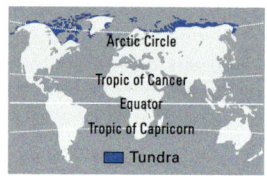

1

2 Tundra landscape

tundra
  Tundra
to adapt
  sich anpassen
shrub
  Strauch
to absorb
  aufnehmen
sunrays
  Sonnenstrahlen
musk ox
  Moschusochse
to survive
  überleben
fur
  Fell
to hibernate
  Winterschlaf abhalten

◄--

Page 12
Interpreting climate graphs

Tundra — the empty land

The **tundra** is an area without any trees which is frozen for most of the year. The temperatures can fall to −50 °C and there are many storms with windspeeds of up to 60 miles an hour (about 97 km/h). Not many people live in this area but a number of plants and animals have adapted to this climate.

Plants and animals

In the tundra you can only find small plants like shrubs and mosses. They grow close to the ground and in groups so that they are protected against the cold and the windy weather. Their dark colours mean that they can absorb more of the sun's rays. Some animals like the musk ox or the caribou can survive in the tundra. The cold climate does not hurt them because they have thick fur and a lot of fat in their body. But when it becomes too cold in winter many animals hibernate or go south where it is warmer and where they can find food.

3 Climate graph Vardo

4 Animals of the tundra

Listening

Norilsk – an industrial ,island' in the Siberian tundra
104510-0306

5 Gas from Siberia

Permafrost

The ground of the tundra is always frozen; this is called **permafrost ground**. In summer the temperatures can rise above 0 °C so that the top layer of the permafrost can melt. Then there are many marshes and lakes in the tundra because the water cannot sink into the frozen soil.

Gas from Siberia

A lot of gas we use in Germany comes from the tundra region of Siberia. It is transported to Germany in pipelines over a distance of 5,000 km. It is not easy to build pipelines in the tundra. The gas heats up the permafrost ground, melting it and making the soil soft. The soft soil can't hold the pipelines and they can break. In the past there were a lot of pipeline accidents and the liquid gas polluted the ground and the water. Today pipelines are built on steel poles.

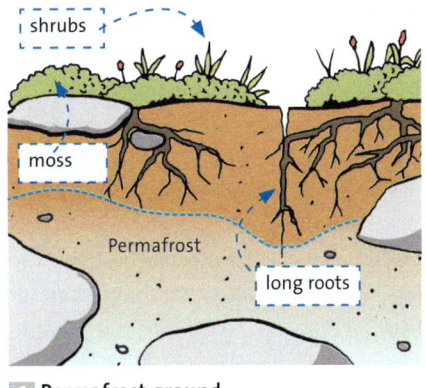

6 Permafrost ground

permafrost ground
Permafrost/Dauerfrostboden
top layer
oberste Schicht
marsh
Sumpf
soil
Boden
accident
Unfall
liquid gas
Flüssiggas
to pollute
verunreinigen, verschmutzen

1 List the countries in Asia, Europe and North America where you can find tundra (atlas).
2 Compare the climate of Vardo (diagram 3) with the climate of your home.
3 Describe how plants and animals have adapted to the climate of the tundra.
4 Look at cartoon 5:
a) Explain why it is so hard for people to work in the tundra.
b) Find reasons why the bear does not like the building of the pipelines.

Cold environments

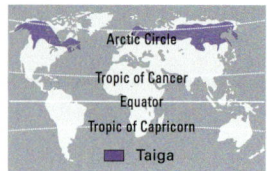

1

2 The taiga, an area full of forests

Taiga – the snowy forest

taiga
  Taiga
boreal forest
  borealer Nadelwald
spruce
  Fichte
fir
  Tanne
precipitation
  Niederschlag
branch
  Zweig
ermine
  Hermelin
endangered
  bedroht
species
  Gattung, Art

When you travel south from the tundra you will come to an area full of forests. This zone is called **taiga** or **boreal forest**.

The climate is too cold for deciduous trees. You only find coniferous trees like spruce or fir there. They keep their needles all year. The thin needles are covered with wax which protects them from the cold. They also don't lose much water which is important because there is not much precipitation. The branches are short so that the heavy snow cannot break them.

Typical animals of the taiga are bears, wolves or ermines. The most famous animal of the taiga is the Siberian tiger. It is an endangered species.

4 Animals of the taiga

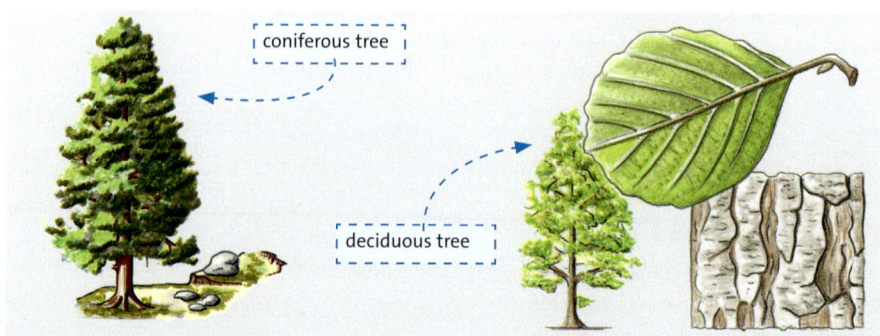

3 Different types of forest

Listening
Ludmilla's life in the taiga
104510-0307

 **Listening**
Depletion of the boreal forests/Protecting the trees
104510-0308

5 Depletion of the boreal forest

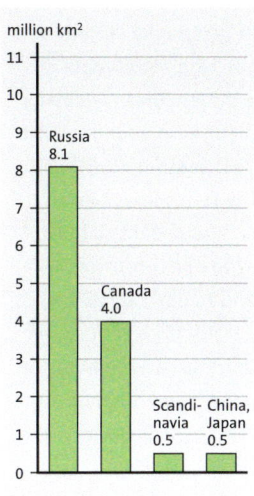

7 Countries with a part of the boreal forest

Ludmilla lives in a small village in the taiga. She talks about her life:
"Winter starts in October. There is a lot of snow and it stays until April. And in December it gets really cold. Temperatures can sink to −50 °C and there is sunlight for just a few hours each day. During this time we can't go outside for very long. If you touch metal, you 'burn' your hand. Sometimes you can even see birds freezing in the air and falling dead to the ground. The only good thing in winter is that it is easier to travel: we can use the frozen rivers as roads.

In May the snow melts and the ground is full of small lakes and mud, so we can't leave the village, only planes and helicopters can travel. We have some very hot summer days, but you can't enjoy the warmer temperatures very much, because there are so many mosquitoes now. I don't know what I hate more: the cold and dark winter days or the noise of hundreds of mosquitoes around my head."

6 Ludmilla talks about her life

depletion
Raubbau
mud
Schlamm

- - ▶

Pages 50/51
How to analyse charts

1 Describe how the trees in the taiga can survive in the cold and dry climate.
2 Explain why there are not many boreal forests in the southern hemisphere. Map 1 can help you.
3 Listen to the text about Ludmilla's life in the taiga.
Describe the problems people have in the taiga.
4 Talk about chart 7.

Cold environments

3 TERRA SKILL

In geography lessons you often work with pictures. There are many pictures in your book, and your teacher often uses them to show things. It is important to look at the pictures closely and to describe all the details. It gives you a lot of information about the people and the landscape where the pictures were taken.

1 Preparing for the sled race

Describing pictures

Have a look at the picture above. The phrases help you to talk or write about the picture. Follow three steps:

Step 1: Introduction
What kind of picture is it?

- It's a photo / a drawing / an illustration / a cartoon / a clipart …
- What's the main subject?
- It shows, illustrates …

Step 2: Describing the details
What people and things are in which part of the picture?

- I can see … / There is / are …
- in the foreground, background
- in the bottom left / right corner
- in the top left / right corner
- in the middle, at the top, at the bottom

Where exactly are the people/things?

- in front of / behind
- above ↔ below
- near / next to / opposite / further away
- left of ↔ right of

What are the people/things like?

- colour: light green, dark brown
- size: large, big ↔ small, little
  tall ↔ short,
  huge ↔ tiny
  round, square

What are the people wearing/doing?

- They are wearing …
- They are standing / sitting …

What's the weather like?

- The sun is shining ↔ It's raining ↔ It's cloudy / …

Step 3: Speculating
What do you think:
Where was the picture taken?
Who might the people be?
Why are they doing what they are doing?

- I think / guess / suppose ....
- Perhaps / Maybe / Probably ...
- It seems to me as if ...

The picture is a photograph. It shows a group of people with sleds and huskies.
In the foreground there is a long sled with lots of clothes and blankets on it. A group of about eight huskies is lying in front of the sled in the snow. Behind this sled further back there are two more sleds with dogs around them. Three or four people are standing around each sled. They are wearing very warm clothes and caps. In the background there is a village with about 60 houses. Snow covers the ground and the sun is shining. It seems as if the people are just starting a sled trip with their huskies. Maybe it is a race. I guess the picture was taken in Greenland because in this country sled races take place.

2 A good description of picture 1

3 An Inuit village around 1900

1 Write a text about picture 3. Follow the three steps and use some of the words from the yellow boxes.
2 Choose one picture of the unit and talk about it with a partner. Take turns: you say a sentence, then your partner says a sentence.
3 Present your dialogue from activity 2 to the rest of the class. Your classmates have to guess which picture it is.

Cold environments

3 TERRA ORIENTATION

You have just come back from a trip to the cold zone. You have learned a lot about Antarctica and the Arctic, the Inuit, the tundra and taiga and even about climate change, a lot of interesting information. This page will help you to structure all the important facts you heard and you revise the key vocabulary.

A trip to the cold zone

Date

Dear ... (name),
This is my first hello from a trip to ... (area, country, city in the cold zone).. I travelled here to... (reason).
I'll add some pictures so you can imagine what it is like here. The ... (first, second,...) picture was taken in ... . It is a really interesting place. However, the region has also some problems. Let me tell you about one of them... (Choose one picture and describe one problem in more detail).

1

2

4

3

5

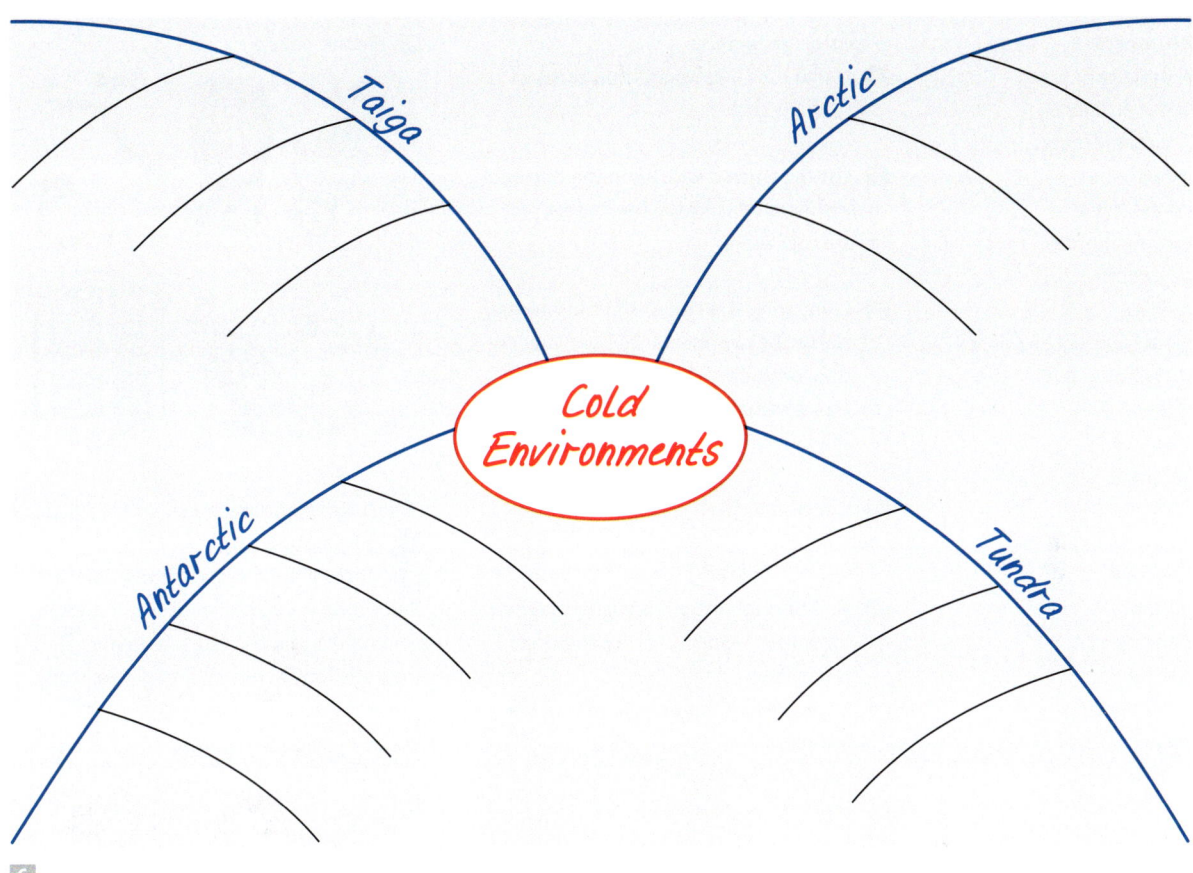

6

Antarctic Treaty,	Inuit,	**to revise**
big melt,	marshes,	wiederholen
boreal forest	permafrost,	
coniferous trees,	research stations,	
continent,	shrubs and mosses,	
depletion,	tourism	
frozen sea,		

7 **Key words from the unit**

1 The mind map helps you to structure information.
a) Copy the mind map into your folder (figure 6).
b) Add the words from box 7 into the mind map.
c) Scan through the unit and add more words and phrases to complete it.
d) Look at the words about cold environments for five minutes again. Then talk about the mind map with your partner. Use complete sentences and take turns.

2 Look at the pictures 2–5 and write down words and short phrases to describe the problem shown.

3 Write a letter to your friend.
a) Copy the beginning of letter 1 and fill in the gaps.
b) Finish the letter by telling her/him about one of the problems on the pictures in more detail.

TERRA TRAINING

Cold environments

Key words
Antarctica
Antarctic Circle
Antarctic Treaty
Arctic
boreal forest
carbon dioxide
depletion
drift ice
global warming
greenhouse gas
iceberg
ice sheet
ice shelf
Inuit
long wave radiation
methane
pack ice
permafrost
pipeline
polar desert
taiga
tundra

Focus on geography

1 Name the three vegetation zones of the polar region.

2 List the three countries in the northern hemisphere which have the largest part of the cold zone.

3 Comparing the size of the continents.
a) Name the continents that are larger than Antarctica.
b) Name the continents that are smaller than Antarctica.

4 Which country does Greenland still belong to?

5 Find the odd one out and give a reason.
a) frozen sea – polar bear – penguin – North Pole
b) Greenland – Canada – Russia – Great Britain
c) research stations – nuclear weapons – tourists – scientists
d) bow and arrow – gun – harpoon – igloo
e) rabbit – polar bear – caribou – musk ox
f) palm tree – pine – spruce – fir

6 Tourism in Antarctica: Make a list of pros and cons.

7 "More global warming, less polar bears." Explain.

Focus on language

8 Find the word.
a) It's made of steel and you transport oil and gas in it.
b) It breaks away from an ice shelf and is very dangerous for ships.
c) North of this line you find the Arctic on a globe.
d) The Inuit hunted seals with this weapon.
e) In this document you find agreements to protect Antarctica.

9 Picture puzzle

a)

b)

Focus on geographical skills

10 Temperature diagram
The three graphs show the temperature lines of three places: in the polar desert, the tundra and the taiga. Say which line belongs to which zone and give reasons.

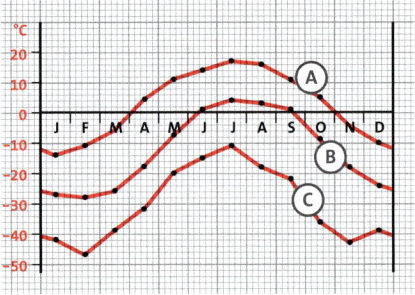

1

11 Describing a cartoon
Describe cartoon 2. Say what problem is being shown.

2

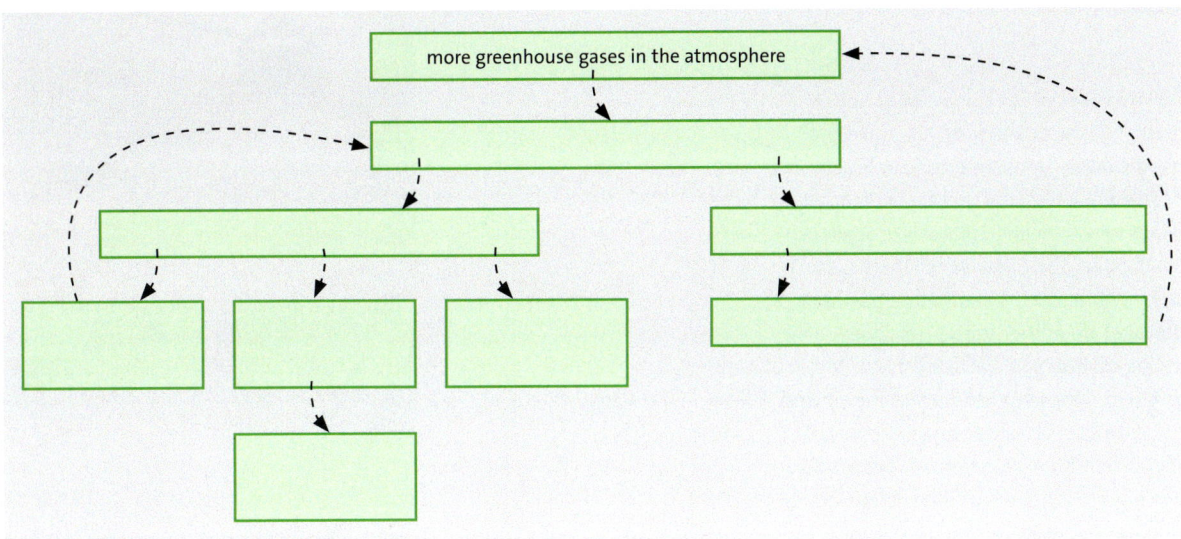

3 Flow chart

12 Copy flow chart 3 into your folder and put the phrases in the right box.

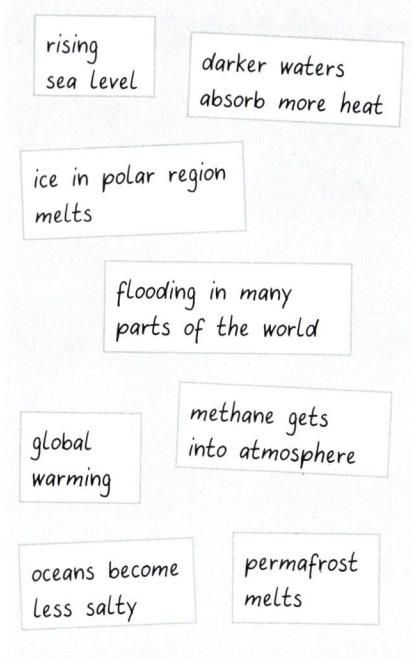

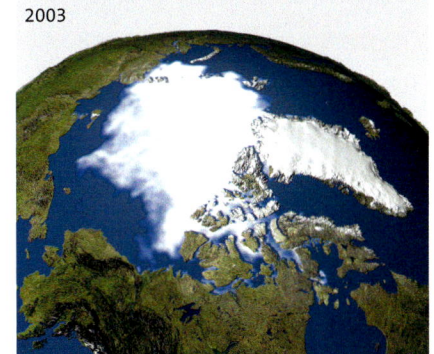

4 Phrases

5 Satellite images

13 Comparing satellite images
Look at the two NASA satellite images (figure 5).
a) Use your atlas and find what out what continents are shown.
b) Compare the two satellite images and describe the changes between 1979 and 2003.

4 Temperate and subtropical zones

Do you know which climate zone you live in? Living in Germany you are in the middle of the temperate zone. A lot of people don't like the weather in Germany. That's why they go to places like Spain or Portugal for their holiday where they can enjoy warm and dry summers. Spain and Portugal are in the subtropical zone.
In this chapter you will also "travel" to different places around Central Europe and see how diverse the zones are. However, there are not only differences, there is also one big similarity which affects both zones: climate change. Have you ever thought about climate change in Europe?

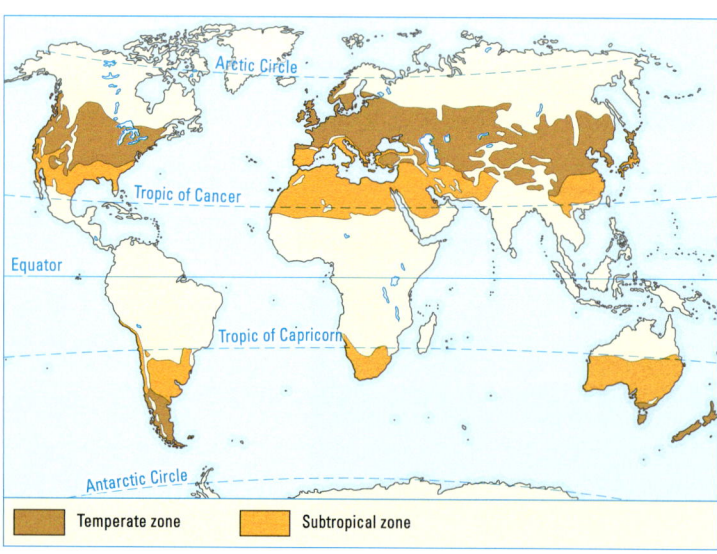

1
2 Wheat harvest in the Boerde
3 Olive tree
4 Dry farmland
5 Flooding in Central Europe

40

Cold in the north, warm in the south, wet in the west and dry in the east

diverse
  verschieden
various
  verschieden
subtropical zone
  subtropische Zone
Mediterranean Sea
  Mittelmeer
to influence
  beeinflussen
maritime climate
  Seeklima
continental climate
  Kontinental-/Landklima
precipitation
  Niederschlag

◀ - -
Page 18
Interpreting climate graphs

Europe is great, not only because it's your home but also because it is very diverse and interesting. There are 23 official languages. Culture and climate are also different. When you go on holiday to Athens in Greece for example you will see that the climate there is different to the climate in Germany. There they have hot, dry summers and winters with a lot of rainfall. This is typical for the **subtropical zone** around the Mediterranean Sea.
The European climate is cold in the north, warm in the south, wet in the west and dry in the east. It is influenced by the sea (**maritime climate**) and big land masses (**continental climate**).

Maritime climate
If a place or a region is near the sea its climate is mostly maritime. The Atlantic Ocean, for example, does not heat up and cool down as quickly as the continents. Temperatures throughout the year are mild. Cool summers, mild winters and a lot of precipitation are typical for a place with a **maritime climate**.

Continental climate
Landmasses can also influence the climate. Regions which are far away from the sea usually have a **continental climate**. The land heats up quickly but cools down a lot faster than water. Large differences in temperature are typical for this climate: short, hot summers and long, cold winters. Due to the dry air there are not many clouds and therefore not much precipitation.

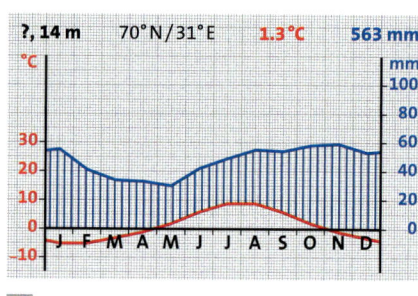

3

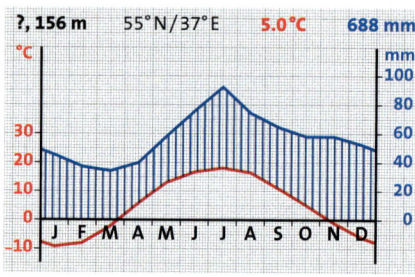

4

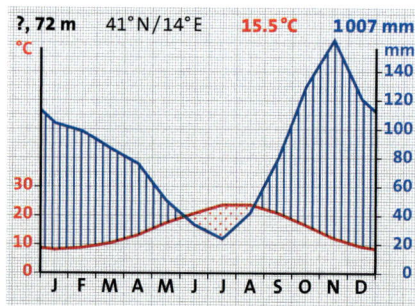

5

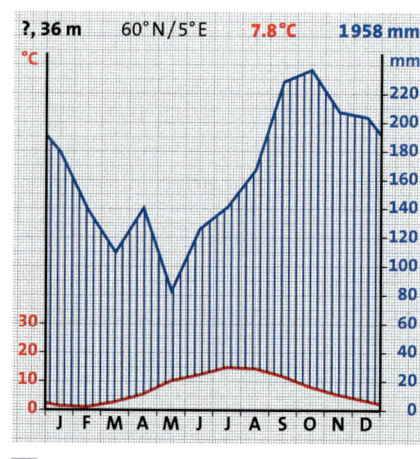

6

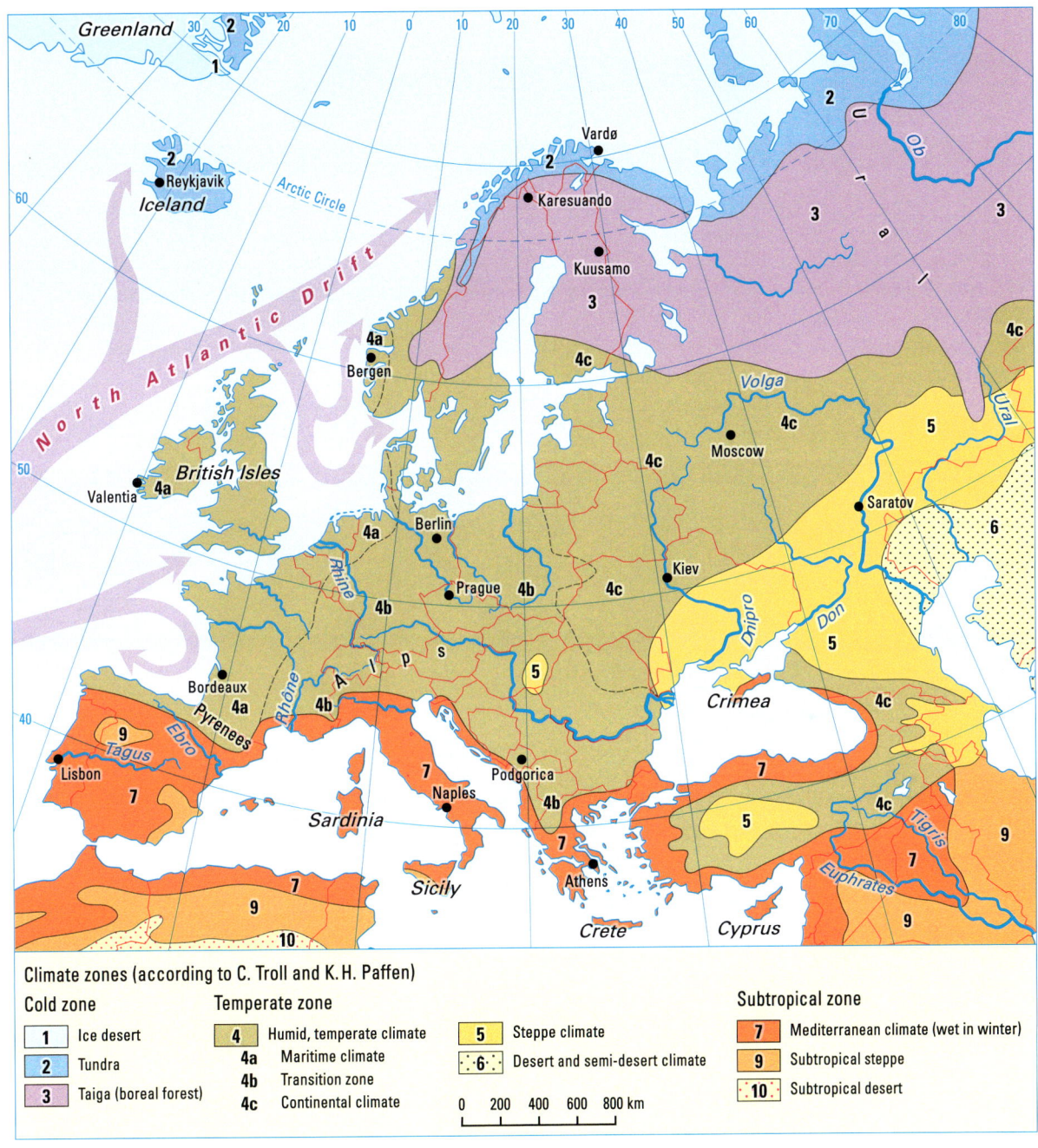

Climate zones (according to C. Troll and K. H. Paffen)

Cold zone
1. Ice desert
2. Tundra
3. Taiga (boreal forest)

Temperate zone
4. Humid, temperate climate
   4a. Maritime climate
   4b. Transition zone
   4c. Continental climate
5. Steppe climate
6. Desert and semi-desert climate

Subtropical zone
7. Mediterranean climate (wet in winter)
9. Subtropical steppe
10. Subtropical desert

0 200 400 600 800 km

7 Climate zones in Europe

1 The four climate graphs show Bergen, Naples, Vardo and Moscow. Find them on the map and fill in the table.

place	Athens/Greece	...	...	...
climate zone	subtropical	...	...	...
continental or maritime	maritime	...	...	...

2 Work in groups of four.
a) Match each climate graph to the right city.
b) Analyse one climate graph and present your results to the class.

Temperate and subtropical zones

1 The Boerde, areas of fertile land.

2 Wind erosion in a field

Gone with the wind...

sugar beet	Zuckerrübe
wheat	Getreide
fertile	fruchtbar
agriculture	Landwirtschaft
natural vegetation	natürliche Vegetation
protection	Schutz
crop	Feldfrüchte
black earth	Schwarzerde
loess	Löss
erosion	Erosion
artificial	künstlich, hier: erfunden

Geography News

12th June 2038

Around 2009 the German **Boerde** was a region where farming wasn't a problem. People grew sugar beet and wheat on fertile soil. This time is long gone. Today the Boerde is an area of dry land where nothing grows. How did this happen? A long time ago, forests grew in this area but the trees were cut down to use the land for agriculture. Soon you could only see fields. Since the natural vegetation was gone there was no protection and people used the land more and more to grow crops. Wind and rainfall took the fertile **black earth** and **loess** away. This process is called **erosion**. Without the soil the land was useless and agriculture not possible. Now it looks like a desert.

3 Artificial newspaper article

What you need:
water tank, a bike pump/hairdryer, dry sand, stones, some grass, stop watch

What to do:
1. Fill the aquarium with 1/3 of fine sand.
2. Pump air into the aquarium with the bike pump/hairdryer. Stop the time.
3. What happens?
4. Put stones and/or grass/plants onto the sand and pump air towards them. Stop the time and make notes.

Results:
Explain your results.

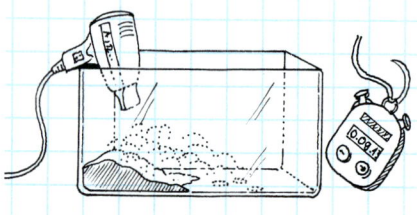

4 Wind erosion experiment

Worksheet
The German "Boerde"—soil from the ice age
104510-0401

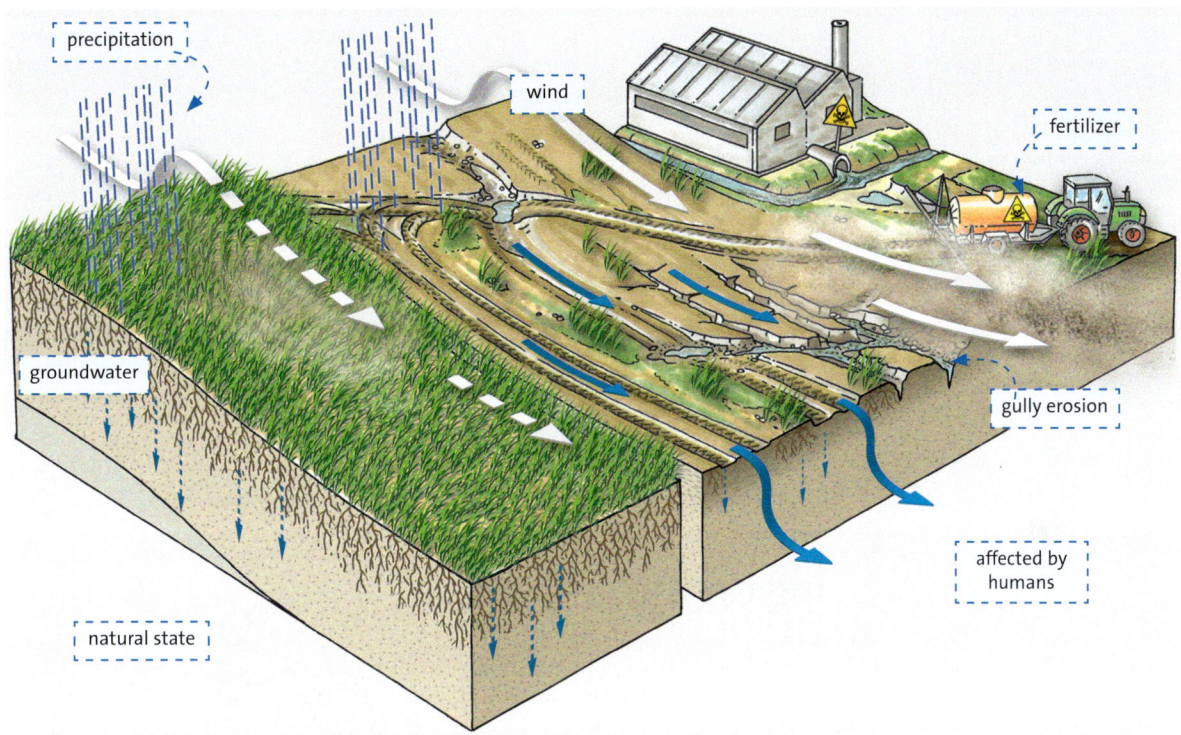

5 Destruction of the soil caused by humans

6 Mulch to protect the plants

state
  Zustand
gully erosion
  Grabenerosion
affected
  beeinflusst
destruction
  Zerstörung
soil
  Erde
mulch
  (Rinden-)mulch
to represent
  repräsentieren
to solve
  lösen

1 Explain the headline "Gone with the wind".

2 Read the newspaper article and look at drawing 5. The example also represents other agricultural areas in Germany.
a) List all problems which are shown.
b) Outline ways to solve these problems (experiment 4, picture 6, Internet).

3 Find other areas around the world where soil erosion is a problem. Present your findings to the class and locate them on a world map (atlas).

45

Temperate and subtropical zones

1

2 Olive plantation

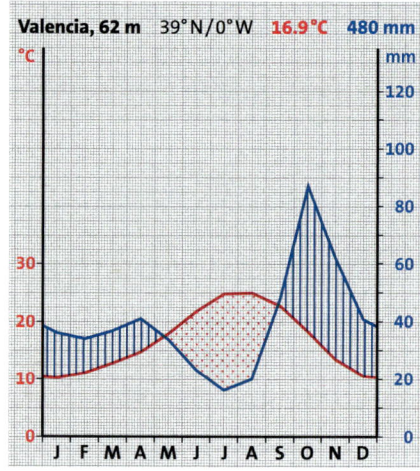
5 Climate graph Valencia

Living on the sunny side

amount
  Menge
furrow irrigation
  Furchenbewässerung
drip irrigation
  Tröpfchenbewässerung
arid
  arid, trocken
to be limited
  begrenzt sein
amount
  Menge
to receive
  erhalten
effective
  effektiv, wirksam
evaporation
  Verdunstung
to waste
  verschwenden

From Easter to autumn many tourists leave Germany for the southern part of Spain. They travel there to enjoy the warm, dry summers and to see the beautiful landscape with its special vegetation. It is one of the places where nice fruits like oranges, grapes and peaches grow well.

However, some people who live in southern Spain sometimes don't like the hot and dry weather. Can you think of any problems they have?

3 Furrow irrigation

4 Drip irrigation

"I like living in Valencia but it is sometimes difficult. Most summers are very arid and we only have a limited amount of water. Some farmers use special forms of irrigation like **drip irrigation**. The plants receive water directly through a small pipeline. It is very effective because only 10–20% of water is lost through evaporation. This method is very expensive though and can't be used by everyone. Another method is the so-called **furrow irrigation**. The water is put on fields in large furrows. However, this method is not as effective as drip irrigation because a lot of water is wasted through evaporation. Another problem is tourism. Of course, the tourists bring a lot of money but they also waste a lot of water."

6

Listening
Carlos Torres talks about his life
104510-0402

 **Worksheet**
Farming in Italy - wine, olives and sheep
104510-0403

Page 50
How to analyse charts:
Tourism in Majorca

7 Different interests

"Two thousand years ago Greeks and Romans destroyed most of the **natural vegetation** in our region. They cut down the old forests and used the wood for fuel and for building ships and houses. After a while secondary vegetation grew back. This is called "Mediterranean scrub" and are low conifers, hedges and thorn bushes. They don't look very nice. These plants have adapted to the dry and hot summers. They often have small waxy leaves or thorns and a thick bark to reduce transpiration and to help them when it gets really hot. They have extra long roots to get to the low groundwater table. In summer the plants are almost inactive"

adapted from: PZ Rheinland-Pfalz (Hrsg.), Brigitte Dreymüller et. al., PZ-Informationen 21/99, Bilingualer Unterricht Erdkunde/Englisch in Jg. 7, p. 62

8 From a tourist guide

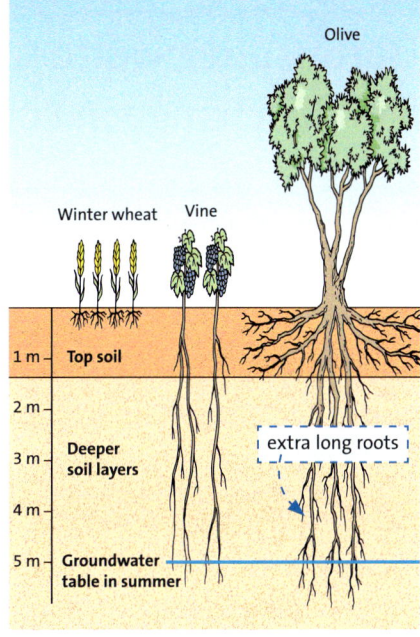

9 Mediterranean vegetation

to destroy
  zerstören
fuel
  Benzin, hier: Brennmaterial
secondary vegetation
  Zweitvegetation
scrub
  Gestrüpp, Buschwerk
conifer
  Nadelbaum, Konifere
hedge
  Hecke
thorn bush
  Dornenbusch
to adapt
  sich anpassen
waxy leaves
  wächserne Blätter
thick bark
  dicke Rinde
transpiration
  Verdunstung

1 A lot of tourists travel to Valencia each year. Suggest reasons why they might choose Valencia for their holiday (climate graph 5, text, picture 2).
2 Carlos Torres said farmers in Spain use special forms of irrigation.
a) Give reasons why they have to use them.
b) Copy figure 9 in your folder. Write down short sentences to describe the Mediterranean vegetation (text 8).
3 Describe the cartoon 7 and name the problem the cartoonist wants to express.
4 Make a list of all countries around the Mediterranean Sea. Name their capitals.
5 Work in groups. Create a leaflet to make tourists use less water. In your leaflet you should:
a) describe the problems of the farmers.
b) name ways that the tourists could use less water while on holiday. Write down short phrase and draw pictures.

1 Not enough water in Southern Spain

2 Too much water: flooding in Hitzacker in 2006

Hotter, drier, wetter and more extreme – climate change in Europe?

climate change
  Klimawandel
scientist
  Wissenschaftler
global climate model
  Klimamodellrechnung
to compare
  vergleichen
glacier
  Gletscher
harvest
  Ernte
to be puzzled
  verwirrt sein

Climate change and global warming are often in the news. The media wants to inform people about the topic. It is hard for journalists to report on climate change because there are still some things about it which are not really understood. To find out more information scientists use a special computer programme called a **global climate model.** Scientists take data from different years, compare them and can then say what might happen in the future.

3 Front cover of a magazine in Germany

◀ - -
Page 34
Describing pictures

1 Describe photos 1 and 2. Use the following terms: drought – floodings– heavy rain – melting glaciers – harvest.
2 Experts say our climate is changing. Make a list of things that could happen (cartoon 4, text, Internet)
3 The Loreley is a famous rock next to the Rhine.

a) Look for information about the Loreley and the famous song on the Internet.
b) Describe cartoon 4.
c) Explain why the skipper in the cartoon is puzzled.
4 Say what you think about the magazine cover 3. Here are some phrases to help you: I think .../I like.../I don't like.../...it is interesting, shocking, boring.

Listening

Interview with Peter Allen
104510-0404

4 The Loreley

For her school magazine, student Tina Mayerhofer interviewed Peter Allan, a scientist from the Centre for Atmospheric Science:

Tina: Mr Allan, the media tells us that our climate is changing. Is this correct?
P. Allan: Yes, that's right.
Tina: Can you tell us some facts?
P. Allan: There are some things that we know for sure. So-called greenhouse gases like carbon dioxide act to warm the earth's atmosphere.
Tina: And, how do you know that?
P. Allan: We found out that the earth's average surface temperature today is 0.6 °C higher than it was in 1900. We also noticed that sea ice in the Arctic and some of the glaciers on the mountains have melted over the last 50 years. This is problematic because melting glaciers mean less water in rivers and therefore farmers might not have enough water to irrigate fields and plantations.
Tina: Oh, and what will our earth look like in the future then?
P. Allan: It is important to know that even as scientists we can't be sure what climate change will bring. However, research shows that global temperatures and the sea level may rise in the next 100 years.
Tina: Will this also change our way of life in Europe?
P. Allan: The simple answer to that is, I don't know how this will affect people, plants, and animals individually. It is possible though that there might not be any winters in Europe. That it will get a lot warmer. Some people might like this idea because they can grow crops they couldn't grow before, for other region this means there is a higher chance of droughts. All these changes can affect the way people live and the way ecosystems exist.

greenhouse gas
   Treibhausgas
carbon dioxide
   Kohlenstoffdioxid
average surface temperature
   durchschnittliche Oberflächentemperatur
to irrigate
   bewässern
sea level
   Meeresspiegel
to affect
   beeinflussen
crop
   Feldfrüchte
drought
   Dürre
ecosystem
   Ökosystem

5 Is climate changing? An interview with Peter Allan

4 TERRA SKILL

In geography you often get information from numbers and statistics. It is much easier to see patterns when the information is presented in the form of colourful charts and diagrams. Diagrams and charts can have different topics and it is important to analyse them carefully.

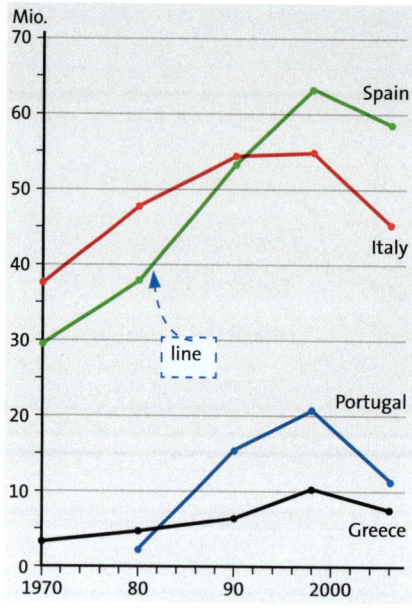

1 Line graph: Foreign tourists in southern Europe

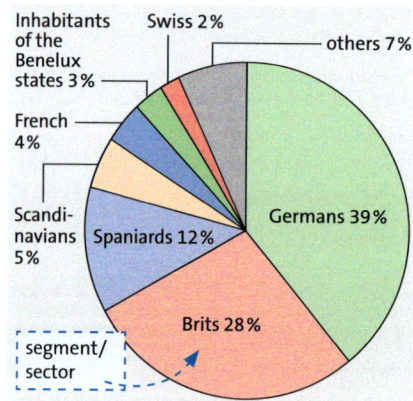

2 A pie chart: Domestic and foreign tourists in Majorca in 2001

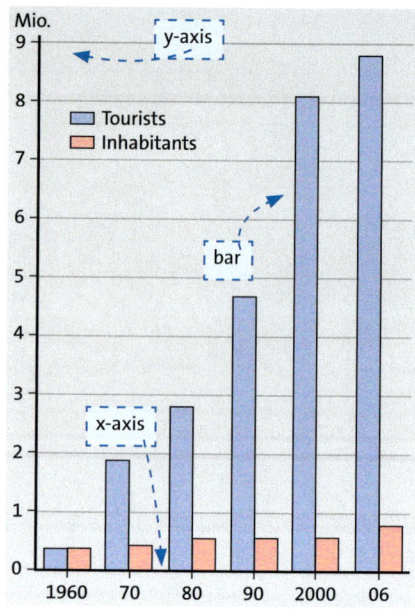

3 Bar chart: Tourists visiting Majorca

How to analyse charts

There are different types of charts, as you can see here. These charts show information about tourism in Europe.

A line graph shows how something develops over time. This one shows how many tourists visited Spain, Italy, Portugal and Greece from 1970 to 2006.

A bar chart compares two different aspects and shows which is bigger (or smaller). This one compares the numbers of tourists and inhabitants in Majorca with each other.

A pie chart shows how an aspect is divided into different parts or sectors. This one shows the percentage of different nationalities of tourists visiting Majorca in 2001.

Follow these steps

Step 1: Description

What kind of graph (line graph, bar chart, pie chart) is it?
What do the title, key, axes, labels, sectors tell you?
What are major changes/differences you can see?

- The chart shows that …
- … remains constant
- More / Less that half of …
- Over / Nearly twice as many / three times as many …
- … reached a peak of …

Step 2: Interpretation

What are the reasons for changes/differences you described?
What are main points/aspects you get from the chart?

- If you compare the figures for … and …, you can see …
- … shows a(n) increase / decrease / steady growth / slight rise / …
- an all-time-high / low

Step 3: Conclusion

What do the results tell you about the topic?
Are there any missing information (research the topic in your geography book, on the Internet, etc.)?

- The chart doesn't say anything about …

This line graph shows how many tourists came to four countries in southern Europe from 1970 to 2006. Italy, Spain and Greece are shown from 1970, Portugal starts in 1980.

The number of tourists increased in all countries. Most tourists went to Italy in 1970, but in in the beginning of the 90s most people travelled to Spain for their holiday. More than twice as many tourists as in 1970 went to Spain and Greece in 2006. Portugal increased its number of tourists five times. All lines show the highest numbers in 1998. Afterwards the numbers went down.

If you compare the figures you see more and more tourists wanted to go to the four countries. This chart shows a steady growth of tourism in the four Mediterranean countries. The chart shows a trend in tourism. Many tourists choose the Mediterranean countries for their holidays. The main reason is their subtropical climate with a lot of sun and nearly no rain during the summer months. The chart does not say anything about the situation in Portugal before 1980. Portugal was quite poor and had to build hotels and streets before it was ready for tourism.

4 An example text for line graph 1

---

pattern
  Muster, hier: Entwicklung
foreign
  ausländisch
domestic
  einheimisch
inhabitant
  Einwohner
percentage
  Anteil
to remain
  bleiben
increase
  Anstieg
steady
  gleichmäßig

---

1 Analyse charts 2 and / or 3 according to the three steps. Use numbers from different years to make your text stronger.

5 Hot deserts – dry climates

They often call the Tuareg the "blue men of the desert" or "masters of the Sahara". Even in difficult times they could survive in an extreme climate for hundreds of years. In this chapter you will learn more about different deserts, their landscapes and how animals and people live in the desert.

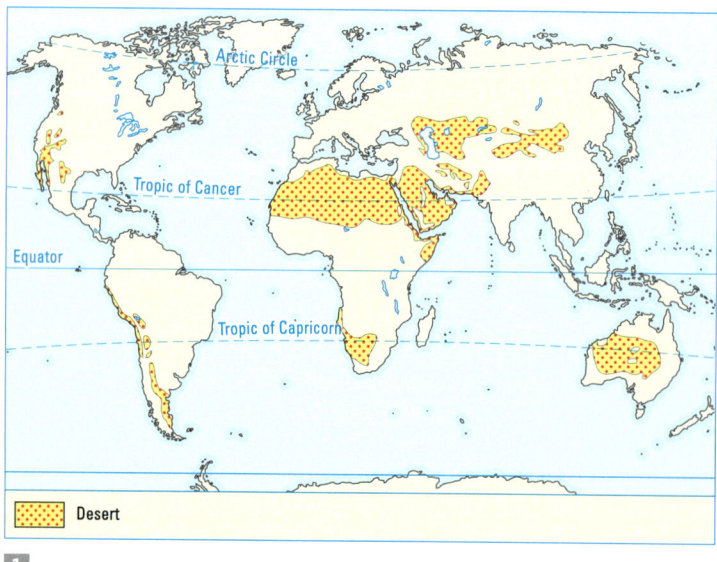

1

2 A Tuareg in a hamada

Desert types

to imagine
  vorstellen
precipitation
  Niederschlag
to influence
  beeinflussen
rain shadow desert
  Regenschattenwüste
lee
  Leeseite (Windschatten)
valley
  Tal
coastal desert
  Küstenwüste
trade wind
  Passatwind
montane desert
  Bergwüste
mountainous
  bergig
polar desert
  Eiswüste
annual
  jährlich

--▶

Page 66
Exercises 1, 3, 5

What is a desert?
There is something magical to deserts. When we think of deserts we imagine hot sand, camels, and oases in a huge area of wide and quiet land. But not only hot and dry areas are deserts, cold and dry areas like the Arctic and Antarctica are deserts too. Deserts are areas of land where there is less than 250 mm precipitation per year. That means almost no plants grow in these areas.

Where in the world are deserts?
Almost one-eighth of the earth is covered by deserts. They are found in every continent and they are all different.

Not all deserts are sandy: desert types
Landscapes are influenced by many factors (climate, vegetation, ...). One can say what type of desert it is when you know where it is:

Rain shadow deserts are "behind" high mountains (in the lee). Most of the Sierra Madre desert is east of the Sierra Nevada mountains. The valley west of the Sierra Nevada gets a lot of rain, but the wet air masses cannot cross the mountains. The mountains stop the rain clouds. This is why some areas "behind" mountains are dry (arid).

1 Rain shadow desert

Famous **coastal deserts** are at the west coast of Africa and South America. They are dry because **trade winds** blow hot and dry air from land to sea.

2 A coastal desert: the Namib

Montane deserts are dry regions in highlands, or mountainous regions.

3 A montane desert in Sinkiang

Polar deserts are areas with an annual precipitation less than 250 mm. Snow, ice, rock, extreme winds and very cold temperatures are typical for Antarctica, a polar desert.

4 A polar desert

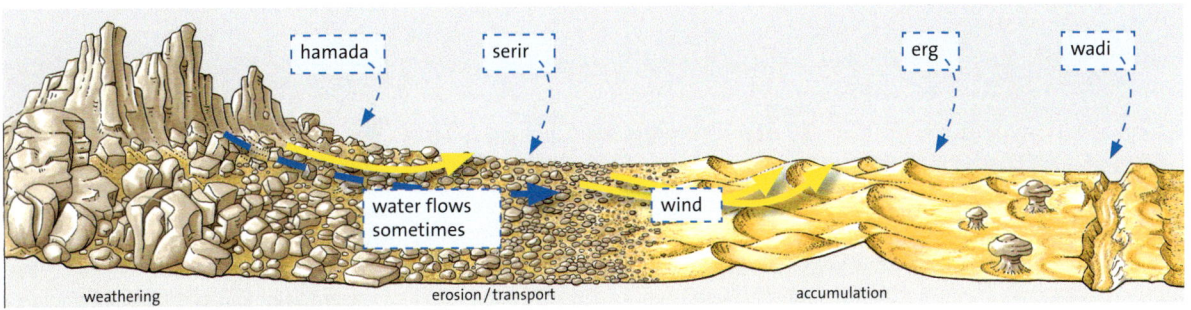

5 How the different desert types form

6 Different desert types in pictures

The Sahara

The Sahara covers one quarter of the African continent and is the world's largest hot desert. Its many different landscapes have Arabic names.

About 20 % of the Sahara is covered by **ergs**, sand deserts. Sand deserts are made of sand which was blown out of hamadas and serirs.

Stony and rocky deserts are called **hamada**. About 70 % of the Sahara is covered by hamadas. How did they form? It is very hot during the day, but cold at night. That means the rocks are also very hot during the day but very cold at night. The change of heat and cold makes the rocks split apart. This process is called **insolation weathering**.

Deserts develop when the finer sand is blown out by the wind. These large areas are covered with gravel. In Arabic they are called **serir.**

Wadis are valleys which are usually dry all year round. When it rains they quickly fill with fast flowing rivers.

erg
  Sandwüste
hamada
  Steinwüste
to split
  zerbrechen
insolation weathering
  Temperaturverwitterung
serir
  Kieswüste
wadi
  Trockental

1 There are different types of deserts.
a) List examples of coastal deserts, montane deserts, polar deserts and hot deserts (atlas).
b) Put the examples in a world map. Use different colours for each desert type. Don't forget a key for your map.

2 Describe how a sand dune forms in the Sahara (figures 5 and 6).

3 Guess how a higher global temperature may influence desert environments (Internet).

Hot deserts—dry climates

overseas
  Übersee
to prepare
  vorbereiten
breakdown
  Panne
emergency personnel
  Rettungspersonal
fine
  Strafe
cacti – plural of cactus,
  Kakteen
to adapt
  sich anpassen
to store
  speichern
shallow
  oberflächlich
to spread
  ausbreiten
spine
  Stachel
to shade
  beschatten
bark
  Rinde

13th November 2008

Too risky: Simpson Desert closed for summer

The Simpson Desert will be closed for the first time this summer.

South Australia's Department of Environment and Heritage said that every year the desert will be closed from December 1 until March 15. Temperatures of 40 to 50 °C are too dangerous for people travelling through the desert.

Director Trevor Naismith said he isn't very happy that the area has to be closed, but they have to. "Some people went missing and we have had deaths in past years in the northern parts of South Australia. Especially tourists from overseas who are not experienced and not well prepared for the very hot and very dry desert." He said that high temperatures mean a higher risk of car breakdowns. "Not only tourists are at high risk. The emergency personnel who try to help visitors are at risk too."

Tourism information centres have been informed. There are information signs when you enter the park. People who cross the desert have to pay a fine of up to $ 1,000.

www.smh.com.au/news/travel/news/simpson-desert-closed-for-summer/2008/11/13/1226318795307.html, © 2008 AAP

Newspaper article adapted from Sydney Morning Herald, 13th November 2008

Life in the desert

How plants have adapted to life in the desert

Deserts are interesting but the climate is extreme. It is hot during the day, but cold at night, and there is not a lot of rainfall. Desert plants and animals adapt to the climate in special ways.

More than 300 kinds of cacti grow in north American deserts. The saguaro (sah-WAH-ro) from the Sonoran desert is the tallest of all cacti. It can be up to 17 metres tall and store up to 5,000 litres of water! Cacti store water in their stems. Their shallow roots spread out to collect rain water before it sinks into the ground. Their spines do not only protect them from animals but also from the sun. Each spine shades the cactus and helps to keep it cool.

Desert plants have developed different ways to collect and store water. Some have long deep roots, others have shallow roots which spread. Some store water in very thick roots which become active as soon as it rains. Thick bark, waxy leaves and spines keep animals away and protect plants from the sun.

Camels are also well adapted to life in the desert. Today Camel rides and races are a tourist attraction, but these strong animals have been the "ships of the desert" for many years.

 **Surf the net**
Aerial video Simpson Desert
104510-0501

 **Worksheet**
Camels' and dromedars' survival skills
104510-0502

 Worksheet
Life in the desert
104510-0503

economy
   Wirtschaft
decision
   Entscheidung

3 Saguaro cacti in the Arizona desert

4 A kokerboom tree from Southwest Africa

5 Climate graph Birdsville

1 Almost one half of Australia is covered by deserts. Write down the names of Australian deserts and describe where in Australia they are (atlas).

2 The Simpson Desert is one of Australia's largest deserts.
a) Compare the size of the Simpson Desert with the size of Germany.
b) Explain why deserts are a problem for Australia's economy.

3 The Simpson Desert will be closed for summer.
a) What is done to stop people from going to the desert?
b) Comment on the decision to close the Simpson Desert in summer. Do you think it is right or wrong?

4 Compare the climate graph of Birdsville with the climate graph of a German town.

	Birdsville	...
Hottest month		
Mean maximum temperature		
Coldest month		
Mean rainfall in these months		

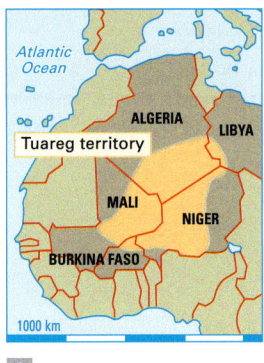

The caravan route from Zagora to Timbuktu was important

Nomadic life – Joining the Tuareg

ethnic minority	
ethnische Minderheit	
veil	
Schleier	
to protect	
schützen	
semi - nomad	
Halbnomade	
trade	
handeln, Handel	
knight	
Ritter	
droppings	
Kot	
to respect	
respektieren	
to solve	
lösen	
to celebrate	
feiern	
sword	
Schwert	

The Tuareg are an **ethnic minority** in North Africa and also known as "the blue men of the Sahara". The men who are older than 25 cover their faces with a blue veil. Women do not cover their faces, only if they need to protect their faces during a sand storm. Their long and loose clothes help them to stay cool and protect them against sun and sand.

The blue people have lived as **semi-nomads** for thousands of years. They were good fighters and very good traders. That is why they are also called "the knights of the desert".

The traditional Tuareg way of life

Women own the house or tent the family lives in and they play an important role.
While men travel through the desert with camels, women stay with the smaller animals like goats, sheep and donkeys. Goats are animals which are easy and cheap to keep. They use the milk and the meat of goat and sheep for food and the skin to make tents. About 30 goat skins are needed for one tent. They even use the camels' droppings because it burns well and that's why they are good to make a fire. This is important because there is not much firewood in the desert.

Nomadic life today

Even though the Tuareg are famous for their camels and blue veils, times have changed. Tuareg don't trade as much anymore as they did in the past.

In the 20th century people build streets through the desert and today people use cars and trucks more than camels. A lot of Tuareg still travel the desert but many also stay in oasis towns and become farmers. Most of them are poor. They are an ethnic minority without a real home country that's why many feel their rights and ways of life are not respected.

In the past the Tuareg met to talk about experiences, solve problems and to celebrate. They still meet but now they celebrate their Tuareg culture. The blue men of the Sahara don't want to forget and lose their traditional culture. The "festival au desert" in Mali is a big Tuareg festival which tourists can also visit. Thousands of Tuareg and hundreds of camels come to this festival. People can enjoy camel races, sword fights, dances and music.

Surf the net
Rallye Dakar
104510-0504

Listening
Salt trade
104510-0505

3 Tuareg selling salt at the Mopti's market Mali

5 A water bag made of goat skin

6 Goats can climb anywhere

goat skin

4 A traditional Tuareg tent

1 You plan to travel with a caravan from Zagora to Timbuktu.
a) Find Zagora and Timbuktu on a map. Name the countries in which these towns are in.
b) Calculate how many days your trip will take when your camel walks 40 km per day.
c) Pack your backpack, list everything you need.

2 Describe in your own words how the life of the Tuareg has changed.
3 The Rallye Dakar is a race which takes place every year.
a) Collect information on the rallye.
b) Discuss why it might be a problem for the Tuareg.

Hot deserts—dry climates

1 An oasis in the Todra Valley (Morocco)

Green islands in the desert—Oases

caravan
  Karawane
good
  Ware, Produkt
to settle
  siedeln
to trade
  handeln
to develop
  entwickeln
crop
  Frucht, Pflanze
date
  Dattel
shade
  Schatten

Oases are called "green islands of life" because there is water for animals and people. Camel caravans with goods have travelled from oasis to oasis for hundreds of years. Both camels and people need water, food and a rest after travelling through hot and dry areas for days. Some **nomads** settled in oases to trade or to farm. Beautiful towns full of life developed. In other places you will only find some palm trees which show that there must be water in the area.

The most important crop of oases are dates. These fruits only become sweet if the date palm tree grows in a hot place with a lot of water. Date palm trees also give shade for other crops. One can use the leaves to make baskets and as building material. This is why Muslims often call date palm trees "the tree of life".

Changes in oases towns

Oases have changed because people built streets to most oasis towns. Now, trucks bring vegetables and fruits. People plant crops to sell them, and buy fruits and vegetables in shops instead. The date is not so important anymore. Many people had to leave their home towns to find jobs in bigger cities. Tourists are interested in deserts and come to oasis towns to go on camel rides. Hotels are built, and often camels carry more tourists than goods.

2 A date palm tree with fruits

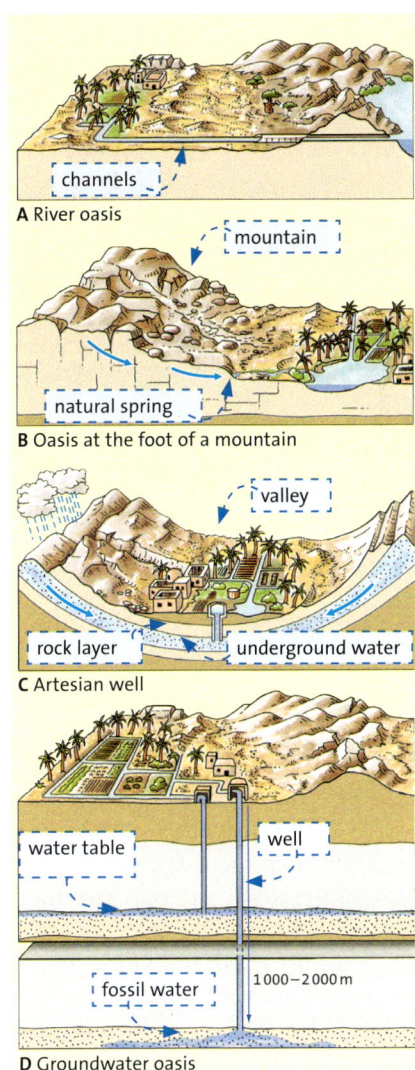

3 Different types of oases

A River oasis
B Oasis at the foot of a mountain
C Artesian well
D Groundwater oasis

a) The oasis is in a valley. Layers of rock in mountains collect the rain water. It flows down the mountains into the valley. When two underground water streams meet in the valley the water comes up to the surface.

b) These oases are along rivers. Water is taken from the river and lead to fields through channels or pipelines.

c) Natural springs give water at the foot of mountains because the water table reaches the surface.

d) The water used is from a deep water table underground. Wells lead the water to the surface. Sometimes these water tables are more than 1,000 metres deep! When they pump a lot of water out of the ground and there isn't enough rainfall then the water is lost forever.

4 Definitions

layer
   Schicht
rock
   Gestein, Stein
stream
   Strom
surface
   Oberfläche
natural spring
   Quelle
well
   Brunnen

1 List reasons why oases are important.
2 There are different types of oases. Match the correct text in figure 4 to the diagrams A, B, C, and D in figure 3.
3 Explain in your own words where the water in oases comes from (figures 3, 4).
4 Use your atlas to look at the following oases:
a) Al-Hofuf Oasis (Saudi Arabia)
b) Oases along the Nile (Egypt)
c) Suar in the area of Tibesti (Chad)
What kind of oases are these?

5 Picture 1 shows an oasis in Morocco.
a) Describe the picture.
b) Find out what kind of oasis it might be (hint: where was the photographer standing)?
6 Many travel agencies offer round trips through Marocco.
a) Choose a tour you like best and explain your decision (Internet).
b) Discuss how tourists are influencing the traditional way of life in an oasis.

Page 34
Describing pictures

TERRA SKILL

Giving talks and presentations are an important skill in life and it is a great chance to get a good mark. When you prepare and give a talk you learn a lot: about the topic, how to organise information, how to present yourself. Giving a well-prepared talk is fun and good experiences make you more self-confident!

1

How to present

To make your presentation a good one you need to structure it the following way:

Step 1: Opening
- Say who you are
- Say what your talk is about

Step 2: Introduction
- Explain your topic in a few sentences
- Make your classmates interested by telling something surprising or special about your topic

Step 3: Main part
- Show key facts and points
- Use visuals (maps, pictures, etc.)

Step 4: Conclusion
- Give a summary about your topic
- Give an outlook

Step 5: Discussion
- Give the chance to ask questions and to discuss some points with your classmates
- Ask for feedback

Let's have a look at …
Let me show you …
I'd like you to look at …
As you can see …

Here …
On the right / left side …
At the top / bottom …

This means that …
This indicates …
This shows …
This brings me to …
It is clear that …
I think this means / shows …
I would like to point out …

I would like to finish by saying …
Let me end by pointing out …

2 Useful phrases

Now it's your turn – Prepare and give a talk.
Follow the task in the green box to prepare a talk in a group step by step.

Group 1:
Oases of Touat and Tidikelt (Algeria)
Group 2:
Urumchi, Hami and Turfan (China)
Group 3:
Nile, El-Harra (Egypt)
Group 4:
Lüderitz, Rosh Pinah, Swakopmund (Namibia)

3 Groups

4 An oasis in the middle of the desert

Possible investors come to your city. They are thinking about giving money to your city. It is important that you get this money to make people's lives better. Prepare a short talk to win over the investors.

Team 1:
Economy team:
You will present the area's natural resources, agriculture and industry.
What is there that they could export to other countries? What could factories produce in your city (e.g. cotton → clothes)?

Team 2:
Sightseeing team:
The investors will only give money if they find out what a lovely place your city is to live in.
To please the investors you organise tours of four of the main tourist attractions and activities. Your city is not only great to work in, your country is also beautiful.

5 Role cards

self-confident
   selbstbewusst
summary
   Zusammenfassung
outlook
   Prognose
investor
   der Anleger/Geldgeber
to win someone over
   jmd. für sich gewinnen
economy
   Wirtschaft
to surround
   umgeben
convincive
   überzeugend

--→
Pages 100 / 101
How to analyse thematic maps

1 Preparation: Form one group for each oasis in figure 3.
a) Locate the town or city on a map (atlas).
b) Name the desert types that surround it.
c) List the crops which are grown.
d) Name the natural resources which are there.

2 Divide your team into two groups.
a) Each team takes one role card. Prepare a short talk to win over the investors.
b) Give the talk. Your classmates are the investors and decide which group was the most convincing.

3 Go through the unit and choose a topic you are really interested in. Prepare a talk and present it to your classmates.

Hot deserts – dry climates

5 TERRA ORIENTATION

A desert is not only a sandy area with high temperatures and camels. You have learnt about different desert types and that people, plants and animals have adapted to the typical climate of the region. This page will help you to remember the most important facts and vocabulary.

Focus on deserts

1

2

3

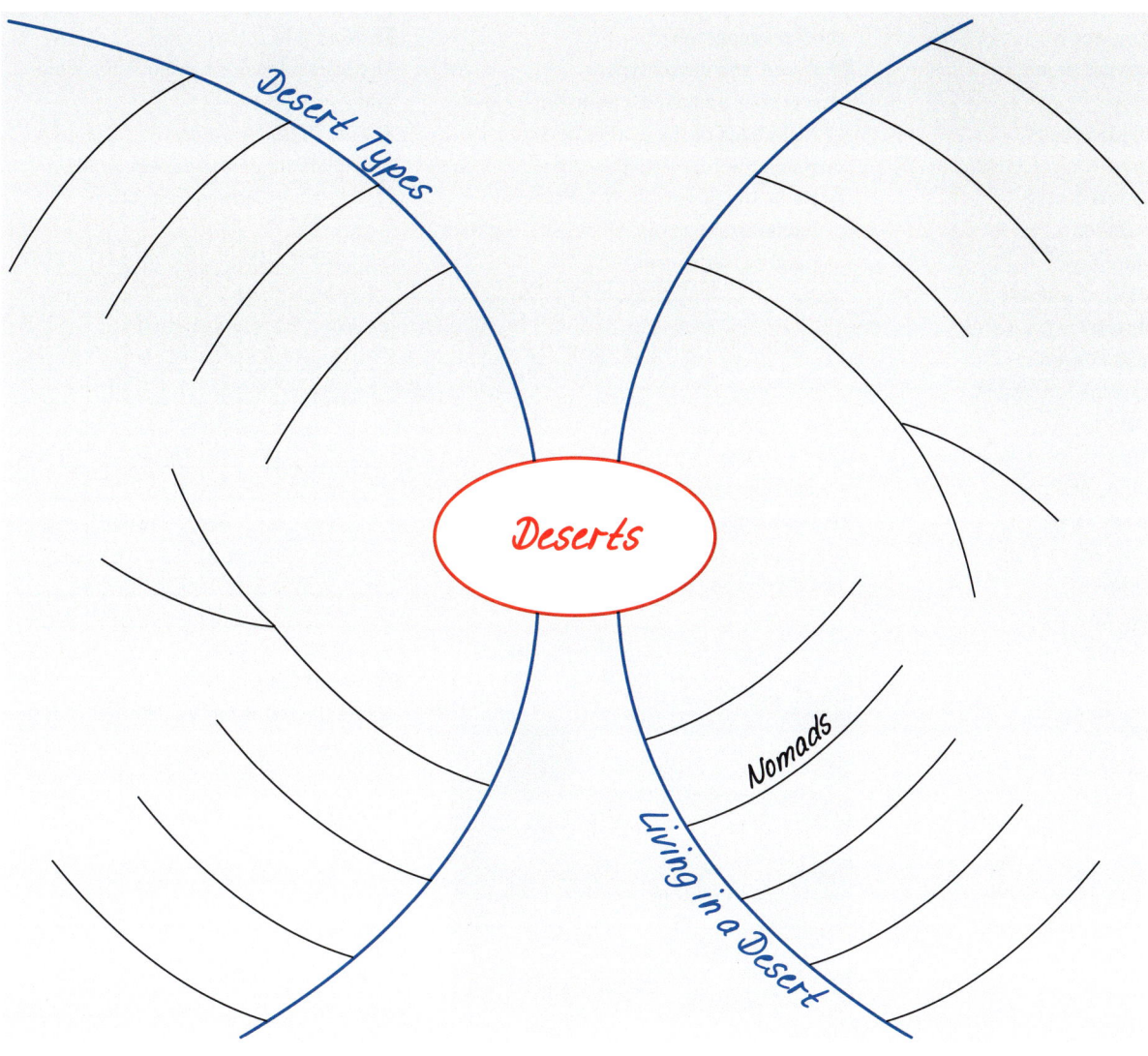

4

1) The pictures 1–3 show different aspects of the unit about deserts.
a) Go together in groups. Think of a title for each picture.
b) Next do a brainstorming in your group and collect words and phrases which come to your head when you look at the pictures.
c) Structure all your findings in a mind map (figure 4). Use an A3 sheet.

2) Choose a topic from the mind map. Create a poster with the most important information and add pictures.

3) Produce a quiz with ten questions about the unit. Then use the quiz to test your classmates.

5 TERRA TRAINING

Hot deserts – dry climates

Key words
coastal desert
crop
dry riverbed
erg
gravel desert
hamada
minority
montane desert
nomad
polar desert
rainshadow desert
Sahara
serir
stony desert
trade wind
Tuareg
wadi
weathering

Focus on geography

1 Desert and desert types

Use an atlas and draw a table (see below).
a) Make a list of the world's deserts.
b) Name the countries they are in.
c) Name the desert type (rain shadow, montane, polar, coastal deserts, erg, hamada, serir, wadi, etc.).

desert	countries	Desert type
Namib desert	Namibia	Coastal desert with ergs
...	...	...

Focus on geographical skills

2 Describing pictures
a) Find out which desert types it is.
b) Describe and analyse the picture.

1

Focus on language

3 Find the right term

The following texts describe two different desert types. Name the desert types.
a) We are at 3500 metres. There is no vegetation on the mountains. The soil is dry and not very fertile. It is windy and a little cold, even though there is some sunshine, too.
b) I am wearing many layers of clothes. Fleece pants and jackets, warm boots, a hat and gloves, and I am still cold! The sky is bright blue, but sometimes it is windy, too. There is ice and snow as far as I can see.

4 Word grid

There are 14 words hidden in the word grid.
a) Find these 14 words.
b) Explain them in your own words.
c) Give their German translation.

	a	b	c	d	e	f	g	h	i
1	A	N	D	I	A	M	O	N	D
2	O	C	D	E	S	E	R	T	A
3	N	A	R	Q	E	A	E	U	T
4	E	C	O	U	R	N	I	A	E
5	I	T	M	O	I	L	H	R	P
6	N	U	E	E	R	G	O	E	A
7	O	S	D	H	O	G	W	G	L
8	M	H	A	M	A	D	A	O	M
9	A	I	R	O	S	U	D	D	T
10	D	T	Y	O	A	S	I	S	R
11	S	A	L	T	T	R	A	D	E
12	O	L	D	I	L	O	E	Y	E

5 Desert types

Name the terms for the different desert types (A–F) on the map. Watch out: there are German, English, Arabic and Berber terms given.
Example:
A: Oase – oasis

2

66

3 ?

7 ?

4 ?

8 ?

6 **Agriculture and land use**
Find the matching terms in English and German for the pictures 3, 4, 7, 8 (dictionary).

7 The following words are mixed up.
a) Put the letters from box 9 in the right order.
b) Write down one sentence about each word.

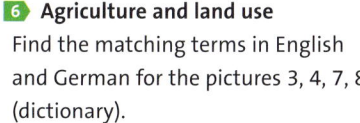

5 **Example (task 7 a)**

Different crops grow in oases.

6 **Example (task 7 b)**

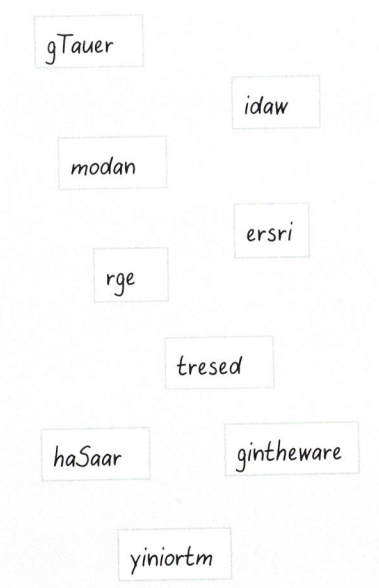

9 **Words mixed up**

6 Sahel, the fringe – Savanna

Most of the savannas are dry and flat grassland areas. The regions are too dry for forests, but not dry enough to be deserts. Savannas have some trees. About one third of the world's people live in these areas. An example of a zone between savannas and deserts is the Sahel. It is located in Africa between the Sahara to the north and the savanna belt to the south. Here, farmers' lives are becoming more and more difficult.

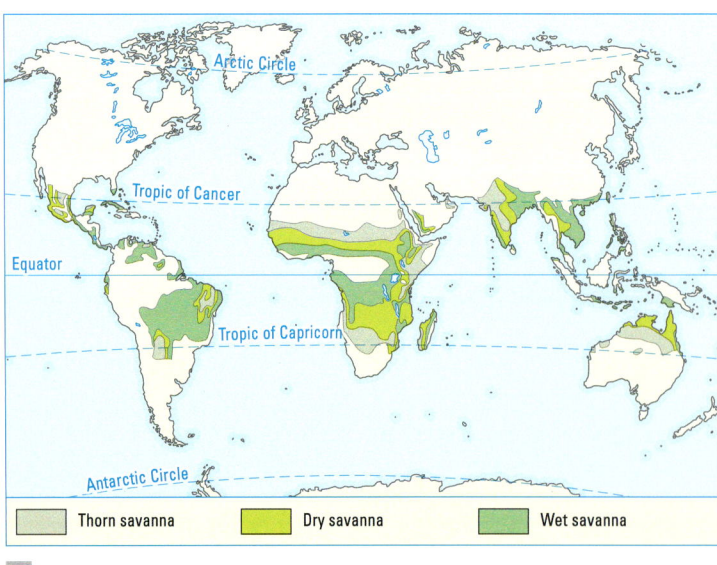

1

2 Different animals in the savanna

1 Savanna in the dry season

Rainy and dry seasons in savannas

rainy season
 Regenzeit
dry season
 Trockenzeit
tropics
 Wendekreise
to develop
 entwickeln
high-pressure area (H)
 Hochdruckgebiet
low-pressure area (L)
 Tiefdruckgebiet
trade winds
 Passatwinde
to equalise
 ausgleichen
ITCZ
 Innertropische Konvergenzzone
zenith
 Zenit
right angle
 rechter Winkel
to influence
 beeinflussen

There are different types of savannas because there is less rain the further you are away from the equator. To understand the reason for that it is important to know how rainfall in the **tropics** develops (see figure 2).

Trade Winds
Wind always blows from a **high-pressure area** (H) to a **low-pressure area** (L). The difference between high-pressure areas and the low-pressure areas at the **equator** leads to winds near the ground. Those **trade winds** blow to try to equalise the difference between H and L.

The ITCZ moves
The sun moves over the course of a year (from the Tropic of Capricorn – equator – Tropic of Cancer – equator). That means the **Intertropical Convergence Zone (ITCZ)** and the trade winds follow the zenith of the sun. Most rainfall is in areas where the sun is in the zenith. In summer the city Niamey in Niger for example is near the ITCZ and

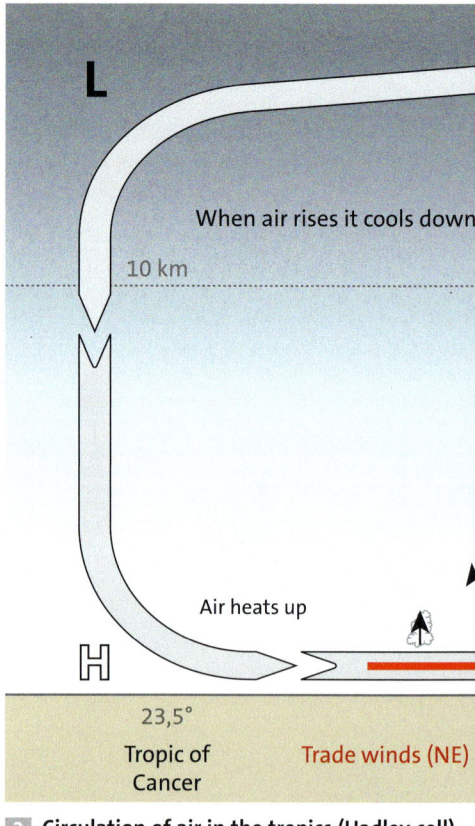

2 Circulation of air in the tropics (Hadley cell)

has a lot of rainfall. In winter the ITCZ moves south and the city is influenced by the dry trade winds. This explains why we have dry and rainy seasons up to 15° north and south of the equator.

 **Extra material**
PowerPoint: Circulation in the tropics
104510-0601

 **Worksheet**
The ITCZ moves
104510-0602

 **Extra material**
Climate data
104510-0603

3 Savanna in the wet season

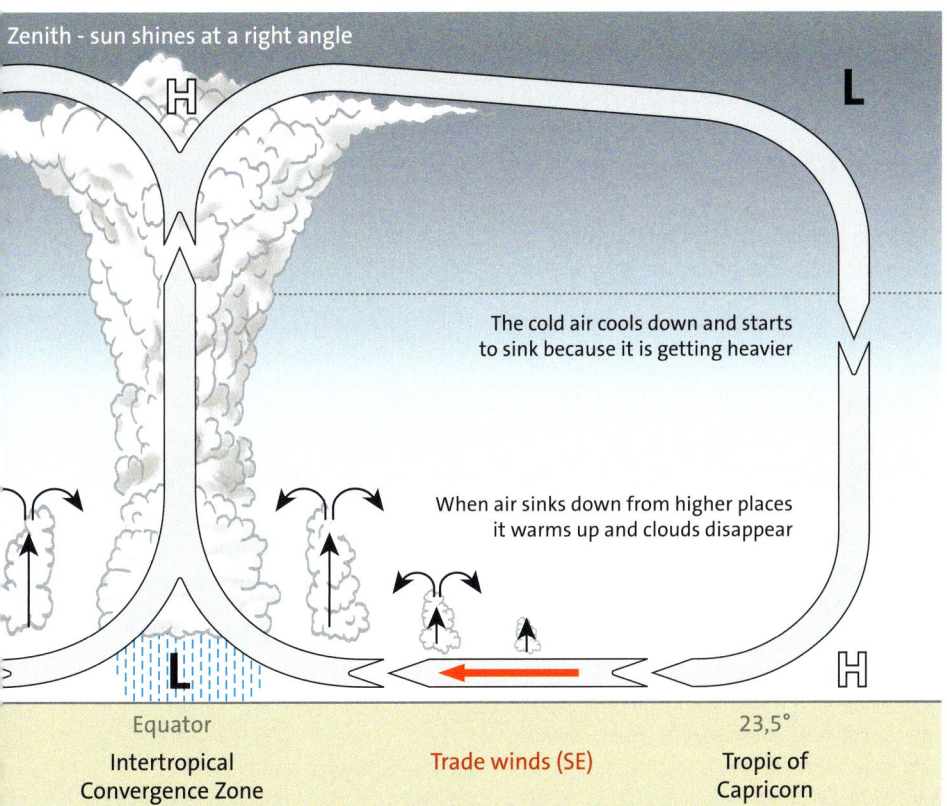

1 ▶ Figure 2 shows the circulation of the air in the tropics. Work with a partner. Describe the processes shown in figure 2. Then explain why we there is a wet and a dry season in savannas (text).

2 ▶ Find another translation for trade winds and explain why they have got their name (Internet).

3 ▶ Put deserts, the tropical rainforest and savannas at the right position in figure 2.

Sahel, the fringe — savanna

1 "Africa's upside-down tree" the Baobab

2 Wet savanna

Different types of savannas

wet savanna
  Feuchtsavanne
dry savanna
  Trockensavanne
thorn savanna
  Dornensavanne
to reach
  erreichen
to store
  speichern
root
  Wurzel
thorn
  Dorne
to protect
  schützen
fire-resistant
  feuerfest
slash and burn
  Brandrodung

The zone between tropical rainforests and deserts is called savanna. The longer the **rainy season** the higher and better the plants can grow. There are three types of savannas: **wet savannas**, **dry savannas** and **thorn savannas**.

Different strategies
The plants in the savannas have different ways to reach the groundwater. Because of long roots, trees can reach deeper water levels than grasses. But grasses have more roots than trees.
Some plants can store water for the **dry season**. Baobab trees for example can store up to 100,000 l of water (a road tanker can only store 20,000–30,000 l!) That is enough water to live for ten months without rain. Some plants have thorns to protect themselves from animals.
Also natural fires can kill the trees that are not fire-resistant. People slash and burn the area to get more farmland. Today, original savannas can only be found in natural parks.

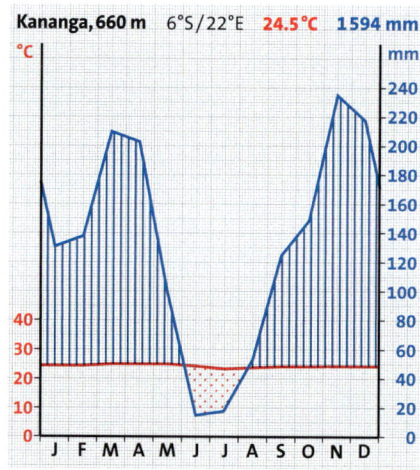

3 Wet savanna
9½–7 humid months
1,000–2,000 mm precipitation

1 Describe what a savanna is.
2 Point out the differences between the different types of savannas.
a) Draw sketches (see sketch 8) of the different types of savannas. Use the Internet to find information like the height of grass or trees.

Extra material
BBC film: Wild Africa – Savannas
104510-0604

4 Dry savanna

6 Thorn savanna

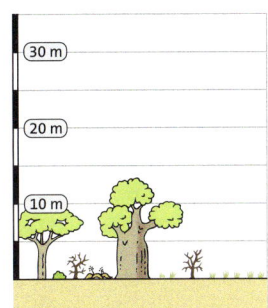
8 Sketch of a thorn savanna

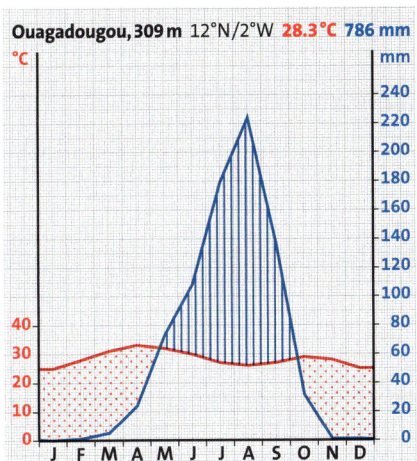
5 Dry savanna
7 – 4½ humid months
500 – 1,000 mm precipitation

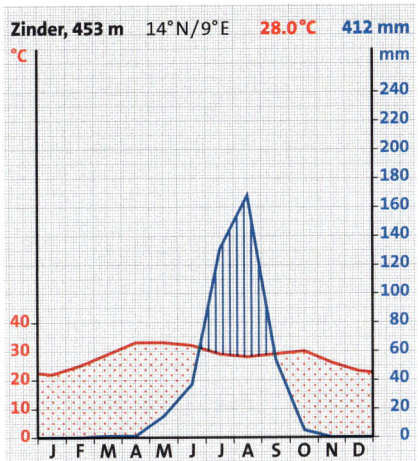
7 Thorn savanna
4½ – 2 humid months
200 – 500 mm precipitation

b) Draw a table:

Type of savanna	...	...	...
How long is the rainy season?	...	...	...
Annual precipitation (in mm)	...	...	...
Plants	...	...	...

3 Name dangers for plants in savannas.
4 Locate ten countries that are in savannas (atlas).

5 Photo 1 shows the Baobab tree.
a) What type of savanna would you believe to find the Baobab tree in?
b) Explain how the Baobab tree is adapted to the climate in the savanna.
6 Illustrate, why the wet season in climate graph 3 is different from the other climate graphs.

Sahel, the fringe – Savanna

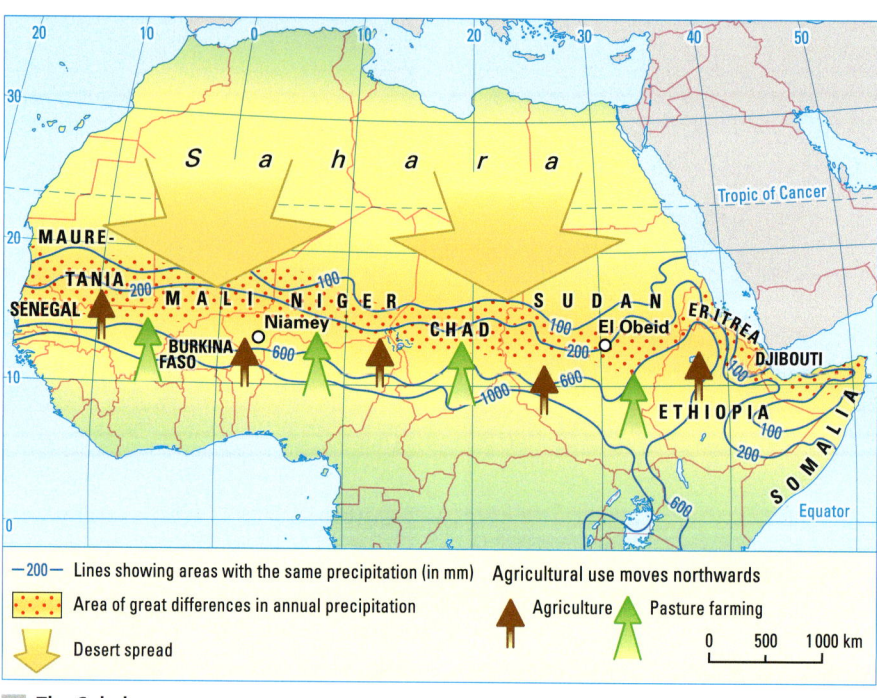

1 The Sahel

Farming in the Sahel

to trade
  handeln
Sahel
  Sahelzone
to develop
  entwickeln
economic
  wirtschaftlich
fringe
  Randgebiet
desertification
  lat. desertus facere = wüst machen
to survive
  überleben
crop failure
  Ernteausfall
drought
  Dürre

Since the seventh century **nomads** have traded in the desert. They called the area south of the desert **Sahel** (Arabic: As-Sahil = shore/coast). After their long trips through the desert they found water and food there. Famous trading towns like Timbuktu (Mali) developed. The Sahel was the cultural and economic fringe between northern and southern Africa. The Sahel has got a problem: the deserts get bigger and bigger. This process is called **desertification**.

Desertification is not only a problem in the Sahel but also in other in other dry areas of the world.

People in poor countries where it is difficult to survive after a crop failure have the biggest problems. From time to time we hear reports about **droughts** in the Sahel. In some years there is not enough rainfall. More and more people and using the land make the problem worse and can lead to more desertification.

2 A main road in Sudan

3 Dead crops on a dry field

Listening
Musa's story
104510-0605

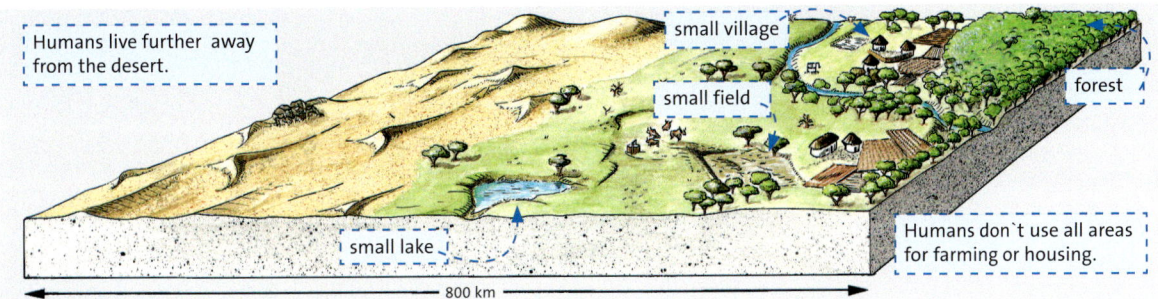

4 Before desertification

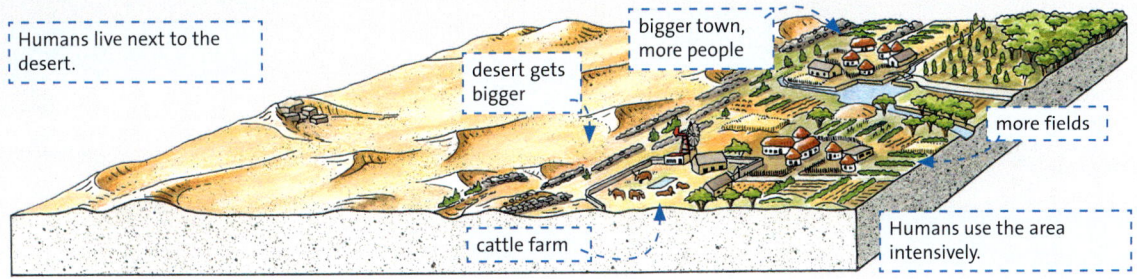

5 After desertification

Musa and his people are **semi-nomads** in the **thorn savanna** of western Sudan. Some of them live in small villages. Further in the south the climate is better for agriculture but they can't live there because so many people live there already. There have always been droughts, but most of the time it was possible to grow millet or sometimes even melons.

When his father died, Musa got many sheep, some goats and camels.

In the dry season, he walked with his herd southwards because it is more humid there. His wife Halima looked after the fields while he was away.

Some years ago there was bad news when Musa came back to the village. There was only dried millet where women had tried to grow something. Of Musa's herd only three goats and two sheep had survived. The other animals died of thirst and hunger or had to be slaughtered.

Some people in his village died from hunger, too.

semi-nomads
  Halbnomaden
thorn savanna
  Dornensavanne
agriculture
  Landwirtschaft
humid
  humid, feucht
millet
  Hirse
dried
  vertrocknet
thirst
  Durst
to slaughter
  notschlachten

6 Musa's story

1 Describe a typical year in Musas's life.
2 Draw a cartoon about Musa and his people. Write down short sentences, too.
3 List differences that you can see in figures 4 and 5.
4 Work in small groups: Discuss possible reasons why Musa and his people live in the Sahel and do not move southwards forever.

1 The desert gets bigger

Desertification

to overuse
  überbeanspruchen
sensitive
  empfindlich
protection
  Schutz
irrigation
  Bewässerung
soil
  Erde
drought
  Dürre
to survive
  überleben
population
  Bevölkerung

One reason why more and more land is is lost to desertification are people who overuse the soil. Some areas like the Sahel are very sensitive to change and then the Sahara desert can move southwards.
How do people overuse the soil? They have too many animals, they farm close to the desert without any protection, they have to use irrigation which dries out the soil even more in the hot climate and they cut down trees. All these are the biggest problems. Because there are so many people, farmers often have to overuse the land – sometimes even during the sensitive drought-periods. More people need more food and animals to survive. The problems will become worse in the future because the population will grow. In Africa for example it's important to have many children that can look after you when you are old.

Help against desertification
People try different things to stop the desertification. At the next page you can find two examples.

2 A farmer on his field

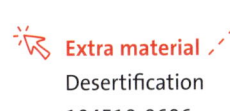

Extra material
Desertification
104510-0606

Zaï against desertification

- Dig a 20 cm deep hole into the ground.
- Put compost into that hole.
- Plant millet in the Zaï when it rains..
- Later, the water is put directly to the plants.
- Zaï is not easy to make because of hard soil.
- Zaï is often successful to make soils fertile again.

Stonewalls against desertification

- Wind is not as fast any more.
- Walls hold back fine material that is quite fertile.
- Only possible in teamwork ⇒ with other villages
- Wind cannot blow out as much farmland and nutrients anymore.
- Walls protect soil from heavy rainfall in the wet season ⇒ less soil erosion.
- Walls made of plants are also possible. BUT: Choose plants that animals do not eat

to dig	graben
hole	Loch
millet	Hirse
successful	erfolgreich
fertile	fruchtbar
nutrients	Nährstoffe
to recover	erholen

3 Help against desertification

1 Farming in Europe is different from farming in the Sahel. List things that are the same and things that are different.

2 Farmers in the Sahel try to stop desertification. Explain what they do (figure 3).

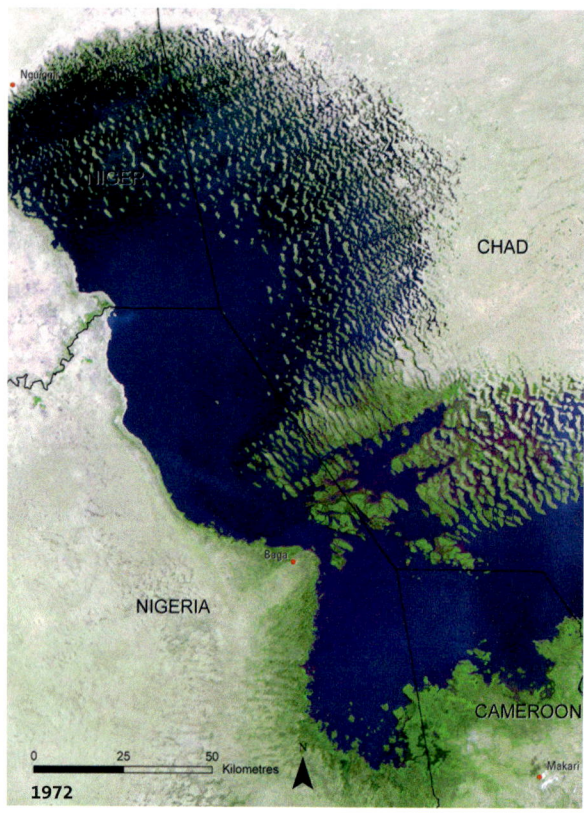 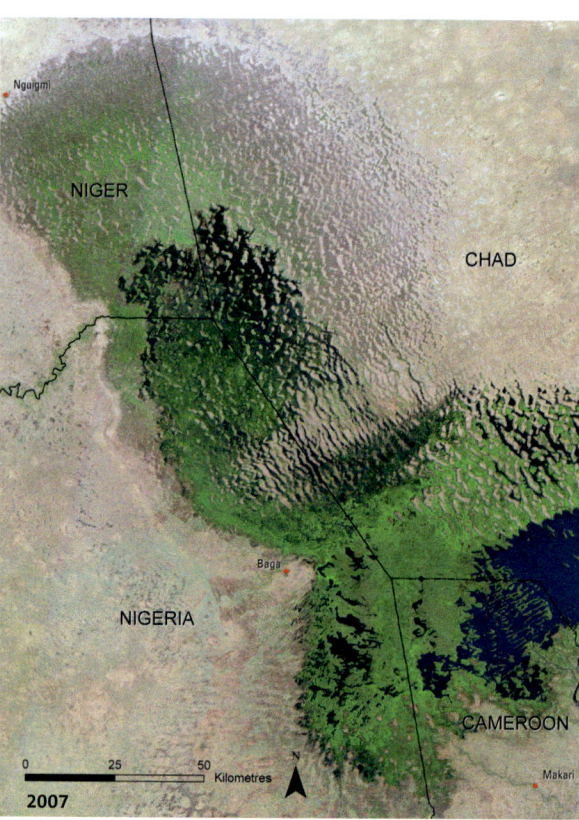

1 Satellite images of Lake Chad

Lake Chad – a disappearing livelihood?

to diappear
(ver)schwinden
livelihood
Lebensgrundlage
freshwater reservoir
Süßwasserspeicher
size
Größe
population
Bevölkerung
irrigation
Bewässerung
crop failure
Ernteausfall
electricity
Elektrizität

Lake Chad is not very deep but it's the only big freshwater reservoir in the Sahel and was once one of Africa's largest freshwater lakes. Mainly because people used a lot of water from the lake, it got much smaller.

Lake Chad in the past and today
The size of the lake today is only 10% of the size it was 50 years ago (although its size has got bigger in the last few years). Why is that? In the northern summer the **ITCZ** moves in the northern hemisphere near Lake Chad. Sometimes the ITCZ does not move far enough north so it doesn't reach Lake Chad. If this happens then there is no rainfall and this leads to **droughts**. The population is growing and more people need even more water to live. Today, many irrigation projects take water from the lake and from rivers that flow into the lake.

Different interests
All these problems have changed the lives of farmers, herders and fishermen. They experienced that there isn't enough water, crop failures, dying animals and fish.
Because there are different interests it is hard to find out what they can do. Fishermen want to keep the water in the lake because many fish died already. Farmers want to use the water for their crops and fields.

Lake Chad in the future
One plan is to take only little water out of the lake. Another plan is to use water from the Zaire River Basin and lead it into the lake. A 2,400 km long canal would have to be built. With the canal, electricity could also be produced.

Surf the net
Film: The future of Lake Chad
104510-0607

2 A farmer in his irrigated field

4 A herder with his cattle

3 Fishermen

1 Look at the satellite images in no. 1.
a) Find out what the different colours in the image show (atlas). List them like this: light green – little vegetation, dark green – a lot of vegetation, …,
b) Compare both images and describe the differences.
c) Give reasons for the changes.

2 Form three different groups: farmers, fishermen and herders. Discuss in class what will be the best solution for the lake. Keep in mind the interests of your group. To collect arguments you can also use the Internet.

➡ Page 82
Fishbowl discussion

6 TERRA ORIENTATION

Sahel, the fringe – Savanna

Deserts, steppes, savannas and polar regions are the dry regions of the world. Mainly because there are more and more people, humans have tried to settle in places where life is very hard. With the help of experience and adaptation they can move but these extreme regions are quite sensitive and when people use the area too much there can be many problems.

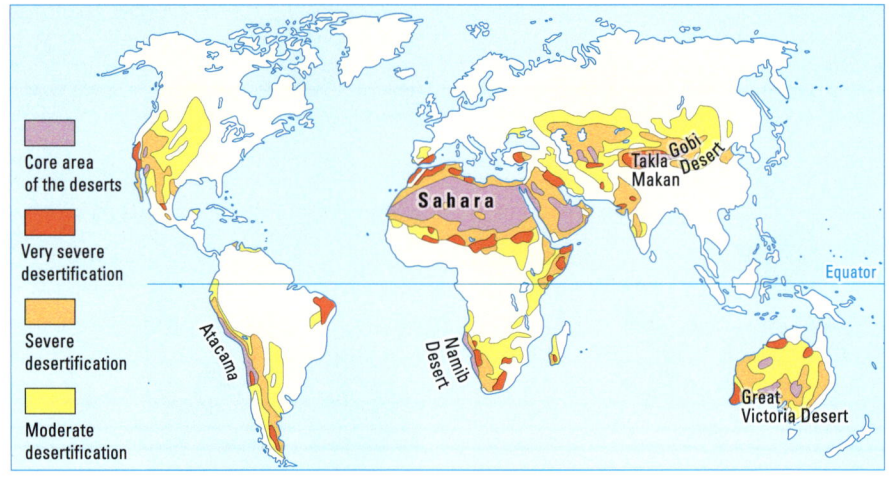

1 Desertification around the world

Focus on: Dry areas in the world

2

4

3

5

adaptation Anpassung
sensitive empfindlich
core area Kerngebiet
severe ernst
moderate mäßig

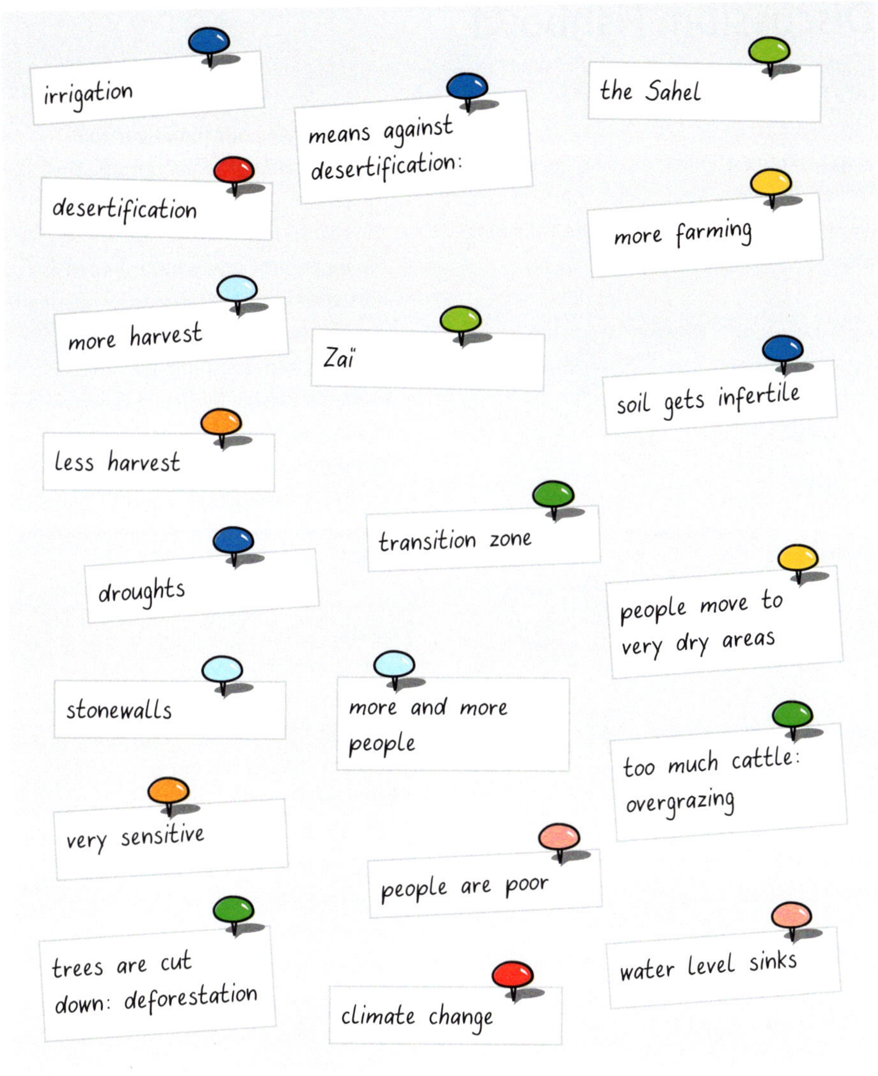

irrigation
means against desertification:
the Sahel
desertification
more farming
more harvest
Zaï
soil gets infertile
less harvest
transition zone
droughts
people move to very dry areas
stonewalls
more and more people
too much cattle: overgrazing
very sensitive
people are poor
trees are cut down: deforestation
climate change
water level sinks

6

desertification
soil gets infertile
= reason
= effect

7 Important words to make a cause and effect chain

1 List countries of the world where desertification is a serious problem (atlas, map 1).

2 The Sahel has a dry and a wet season.

a) Explain where the ITCZ is located when there is the wet season in the Sahel.

b) Where is the ITC in the dry season of the Sahel?

3 Find headlines for each of the photos 2–5.

4 Draw a cause and effect chain (see fig. 7). The boxes above (fig.6) and the pictures may help you. Add own ideas,too.

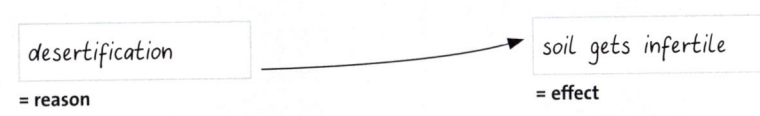

TERRA SKILL

In many discussions the loudest person says most – and the others don't get the chance to say anything.
Have you ever been in such a situation?
Here, you will learn that it can also be different. The "fishbowl" is a good way to have a discussion. "Fishbowl"? – Goldfish live in a fishbowl. How can a discussion be in there?

Discussion: Fishbowl

Let's take a closer look at it:

Step 1: Preparation
For each group that takes part in the discussion put the chairs in the following way:

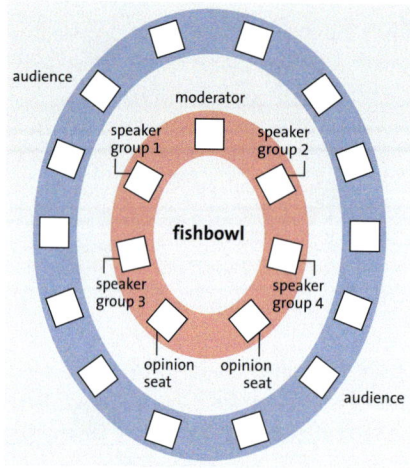

1 Position of the chairs

Step 2: Role of the chairs
Inner circle (red):
– one chair is for the moderator
– one chair is for a speaker of each group
– two empty "opinion chairs" for the other people taking part

Outer circle (blue):
– these chairs are for the other pupils
– they can take part in the discussion if they have something important to say, but only if they sit down on an "opinion chair"

Step 3: Carrying out the discussion
– one speaker of each group and the moderator sit down in the fishbowl
– the two "opinion chairs" are empty
– the moderator says what the topic is
– now each group can give their opinion in a short statement
– students from the audience can take part in the discussion by sitting down on one of the two "opinion chairs"
– the moderator leads the discussion and can decide who has to leave the fishbowl
– you can sit down on a free "opinion chair" as often as you like

I agree
  Ich stimme zu. / Ich bin deiner Meinung.
I disagree.
  Ich bin anderer Meinung.
I don't think so.
  Das finde ich nicht.
I think so, too.
  Das finde ich auch.
In my opinion …
  Meiner Meinung nach…
I can see your point, but …
  Ich verstehe dein Argument, aber…
I think you are right / wrong.
  Ich denke du hast Recht/Unrecht.
That's one way of looking at it.
  So kann man es auch sehen.
I don't get it.
  Das verstehe ich nicht.
on the one hand …,
  einerseits
on the other hand …
  andererseits
I don't think that's relevant.
  Das finde ich nicht wichtig.
I'm not sure.
  Ich bin mir nicht sicher.

3 Phrases to help you in a discussion

Listening
Scandal in Chad
104510-0608

A big European company wants to build a new farm near Lake Chad. They plan to plant crops to sell them on the European market (cash crops). They want to use water from the lake.

Group A
You are a politician from Chad. You like this idea because you hope that it will bring money and jobs to your country. Find arguments in your group to convince the fishermen and the Greenpeace activists that the farm must be built.

Group B
You are the European company. Find arguments in your group to convince the fishermen and the Yanomami of your plan.

Group C
You are the fishermen. You don't like the idea, because it destroys your country. Find arguments to convince the European company and Chad's government not to build a farm for cash crops.

Group D
You are the Greenpeace activists. You don't like the idea. Lake Chad must be saved, because it is an important ecosystem and important for many beautiful plants and animals. Find arguments in your group to convince the European company and Chad's government not to build a farm for cash crops.

4 Role cards

Chad Daily

Scandal In Chad
N'Djamena.: Politicians of Chad's government explained that the European Fruit and Vegetable Company plans to build a new farm near Lake Chad. They plan to plant cash crops to sell them on the European market. The temperatures in Chad seem to be perfect for this project, but they don't have enough rainfall.
The politicians said that this will not be a problem, because the European Fruit and Vegetable Company will be allowed to take water from Lake Chad and use it to irrigate their plantations. In the last few years the water levels have risen again, so there shouldn't be any problems.
Fishermen say that this will put an end to their livelihoods, because the water levels will sink dramatically and most of the fish will die. Greenpeace activists also don't like this idea because the ecosystem of Lake Chad will be destroyed forever.

5 Newspaper article (artificial)

1 Read the newspaper article "Scandal in Chad". Explain what the article is about in your own words.
2 Get together in four groups (A–D).
a) Find arguments that support your opinion.
b) Think of possible counter arguments.
3 Decide on a group speaker. He or she takes notes on a piece of paper to give a statement in the beginning of the fishbowl discussion.

statement
  Darlegung, Begründung
to convince somebody of
  jemanden von etw. überzeugen
government
  Regierung
to destroy
  zerstören
to irrigate
  bewässern
to rise
  ansteigen
livelihood
  Lebensgrundlage
artificial
  künstlich
counter argument
  Gegenargument

Pages 78 / 79
Information on Lake Chad

7 Very wet and very hot – Tropical rainy climates

The rainforests of our earth are exciting – there are so many different animals in a fascinating environment. This chapter will take you on a journey through the tropical rainy climates.

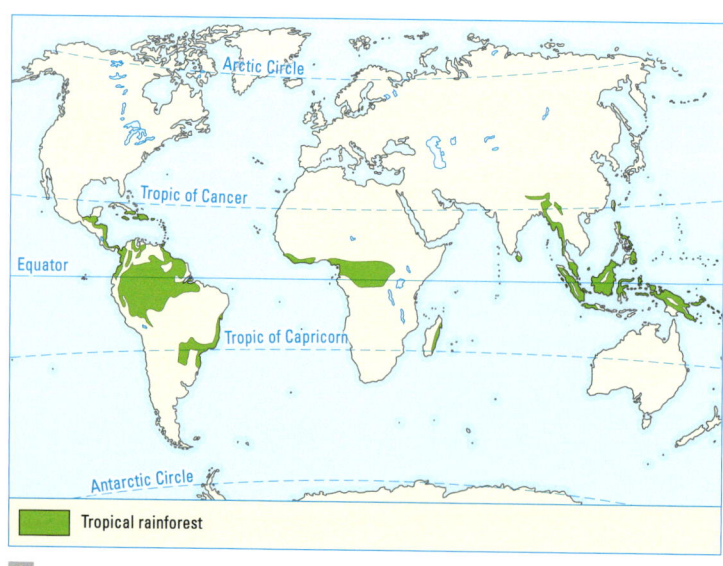

1

2 The Amazon rainforest

7 Very wet and very hot — tropical rainy climates

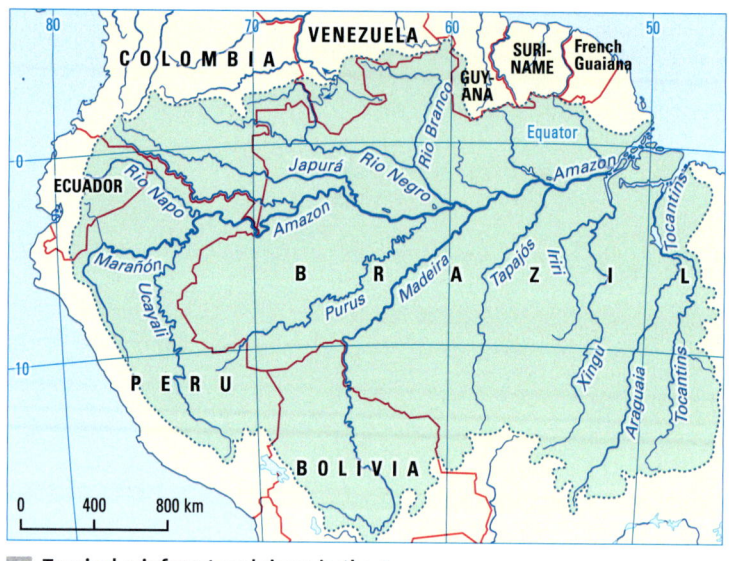

1 Tropical rainforest and rivers in the Amazon

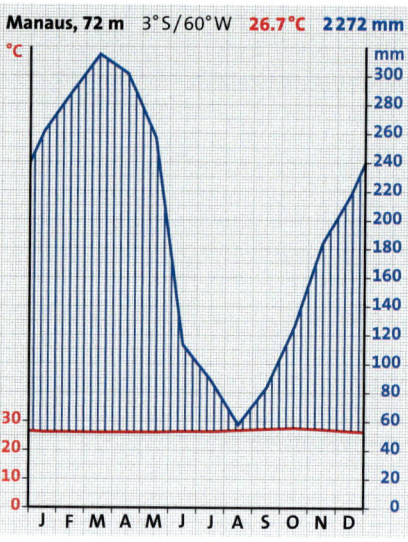

3 Climate graph of Manaus

Making holidays in a tropical resort

humid
   feucht
sloth
   Faultier
skyscraper
   Hochhaus
to be connected
   mit etwas verbunden sein
footpath
   Fußweg
stilt
   Stelze
boots
   Stiefel
to bite
   beissen
animal species
   Tierarten

--→

Page 102
Exercises 1, 6

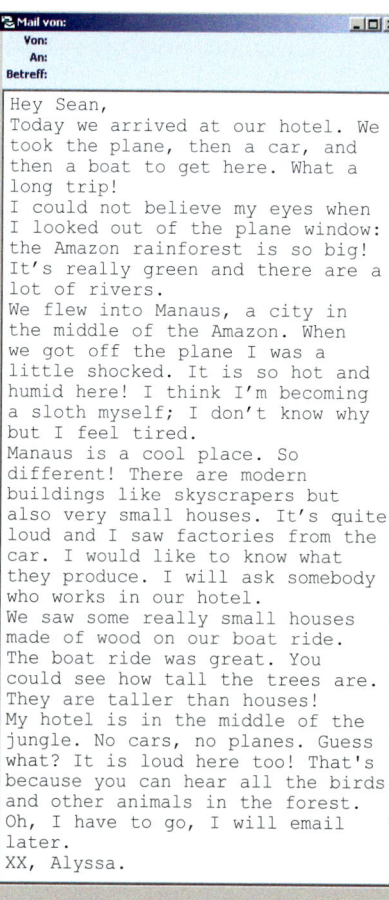

Hey Sean,
Today we arrived at our hotel. We took the plane, then a car, and then a boat to get here. What a long trip!
I could not believe my eyes when I looked out of the plane window: the Amazon rainforest is so big! It's really green and there are a lot of rivers.
We flew into Manaus, a city in the middle of the Amazon. When we got off the plane I was a little shocked. It is so hot and humid here! I think I'm becoming a sloth myself; I don't know why but I feel tired.
Manaus is a cool place. So different! There are modern buildings like skyscrapers but also very small houses. It's quite loud and I saw factories from the car. I would like to know what they produce. I will ask somebody who works in our hotel.
We saw some really small houses made of wood on our boat ride. The boat ride was great. You could see how tall the trees are. They are taller than houses!
My hotel is in the middle of the jungle. No cars, no planes. Guess what? It is loud here too! That's because you can hear all the birds and other animals in the forest.
Oh, I have to go, I will email later.
XX, Alyssa.

2 Alyssa's first email

Hey Sean,
Thanks for your email. It's good to hear from you.
I looked around the hotel more. The buildings are connected to each other with footpaths. The footpaths are on stilts. You walk high above the ground. This way you can see more of the trees, flowers and plants. It is also less dangerous. There are all kinds of animals on the ground which can hurt you like snakes. I am a little bit scared now, but Nenita told me not to worry. She works in the hotel and knows a lot about the Amazon. She said we should always wear boots. Animals on the ground cannot bite through the boots. We should also pay attention to where we step.
Tomorrow we will do a wilderness walk and learn about all the plants and animals! Nenita said that more than 30 million species of insects live in the rainforest. Half of the world's animal species live there, too. Isn't that crazy?
XX, Alyssa.

4 Alyssa's second email

5 Amazon leaf frog

7 Boa constrictor

*Curupira's wilderness tours
– we show you the rainforest! –*

- Free pick up at your hotel: we take you into the forest by boat
- Experienced guides:
  Information about plants and animals
  Make animal noises to attract amazing animals
- Tips about what to wear and how to act in the rainforest
- Lunch and drinks included – in our wilderness base in the tree canopy!

Book a tour with us at the hotel reception or in the tourist information centre in Manaus.

6 A trip to the rainforest

pick up
   Abholung
to be experienced
   erfahren sein
guide
   Fremdenführer
to attract
   anziehen
to be included
   inbegriffen
base
   Station
tree canopy
   Baumkronen
to measure
   messen

1 Measure the size of the the Amazon. How much of Europe could it cover (atlas)?

2 Interpret the climate graph of Manaus (fig. 3). Explain what makes Alyssa so tired.

3 Alyssa talks about dangerous animals on the ground.
a) Describe how people try to protect themselves from animals on the ground.
b) Look at map 1 of the Amazon river system and the pictures of some rainforest animals. Think of three dangerous rainforest animals which live close to the ground.

4 Find arguments for and against going on holiday to a rainforest.

◀ - -
Pages 18 / 19
Interpreting climate graphs

- - ▶
Page 119
Climate data Manaus

Very wet and very hot – Tropical rainy climates

1 The Amazon rainforest

A dense, green and tall forest

dense
  dicht
layer
  Schicht
roof
  Dach
canopy layer
  Kronendach
lizard
  Eidechse
emergent layer
  Schicht der Baumriesen
understorey layer
  untere Baumschicht
orchid
  Orchidee
fern
  Farn
to wrap
  umwickeln
forest floor
  Waldboden
ground layer
  Bodenschicht
humidity
  (Luft-) Feuchtigkeit
noise
  Geräusch

We all know that the rainforest is very special. But did you know that some rainforest trees are 60 metres tall? Tropical rainforests have different layers. Alyssa saw a big green forest from the plane. The trees grow so close to each other that they form a big green "roof".

The "roof" of the rainforest is called **canopy layer**. There is lots of life in the tree canopy. Birds, monkeys, butterflies, sloths, lizards and many other animals live there. Only a few trees are taller than the trees of the canopy layer. These trees are in the **emergent layer**.

Smaller and younger trees, and bushes grow in the **understorey layer**. This is where you can find popular house plants like orchids and ferns. Lianas wrap themselves around other trees to reach the canopy layer. They can be more than 1,000 metres long! The **forest floor** is in the **ground layer**. Because the canopy layer is so dense and high not a lot of light reaches the ground. Only 5 percent of sunlight reaches the forest floor. Jaguars and tapirs and many insects live in the dark and humid ground layer.

Alyssa met a professor from the University of London. This is what he explained to her: "See, the sun only shines on the very tall trees. It is hotter in the canopy layer than in the understorey layer. It rains every day and the humidity in the layers under the tree canopy cannot get out. That's why it is so humid in the understorey and the ground layers.

You say there are many noises in the rainforest. Well, again the dense forest is the reason for this. There are so many plants and trees that the animals cannot see far. That's why they make noises; they talk to each other."

2 What the expert says

3 A squirrel monkey

Listening
What the expert says
104510-0701

 **Surf the net**
Fact sheets: Animals in the layers of the rainforest
104510-0702

4 The different layers in the tropical rainforest

5 A sloth

6 A tapir

7 A liana

to add
  addieren
height
  die Größe, Höhe

1 Look at figure 4 which shows the different layers in a tropical rainforest.
a) Find out how tall the trees are in each of the four layers are.
b) Measure how tall you and your classmates are. Do some maths: add all your heights. Which layer could you reach?

2 Nenita said that the rainforest is home to a lot of animal species. Name four rainforest animals you know. Say in which of the layers they live.

3 Compare the different layers in the rainforest with a forest you know in Germany. Draw a sketch like figure 4 for a German forest. Say what's different.

89

1 Tikal National Park Guatemala

endangered species
  vom Aussterben bedrohte Tiere
strangler
  Würgerpflanze
soil
  Boden
fertile
  fruchtbar
nutrient
  Nährstoff
climber
  Kletterpflanze
epiphyte
  Aufsitzerpflanze
thief
  Dieb
to wrap
  umwickeln
to destroy
  zerstören

Special plants and endangered species

Stranglers, parasites, and others: "Criminal" plants in the rainforest

Look at the picture from Guatemala (picture 1). Isn't this a beautiful tree? But it seems that there is not only a tree – there are a lot of other plants too! Why is that? The soil in the rainforest is not very fertile. That means that there are not many nutrients. There is also not a lot of sunlight in the lower levels of the rainforest. Plants and trees had to find ways to get nutrients and sunlight. Here you can read about some of the "criminal" plants:

Climbers: they are not criminal, only lazy. They have roots in the ground but use trees to climb towards the sunlight.
Epiphytes: they don't have roots and grow on trunks and branches. There they can get more light than on the ground.
Parasites: these plants are thieves. They grow at the bottom of trees and use the tree's roots to get nutrients.
Stranglers: these plants are murderers. They wrap themselves around the tree trunk and kill it.

2 Different types of "criminal" plants

Endangered species
We talked about many interesting plants and animals. People also use the rainforest and destroy it. When forests are destroyed, plants die and animals do not find food anymore. They are in danger because they will die of hunger.

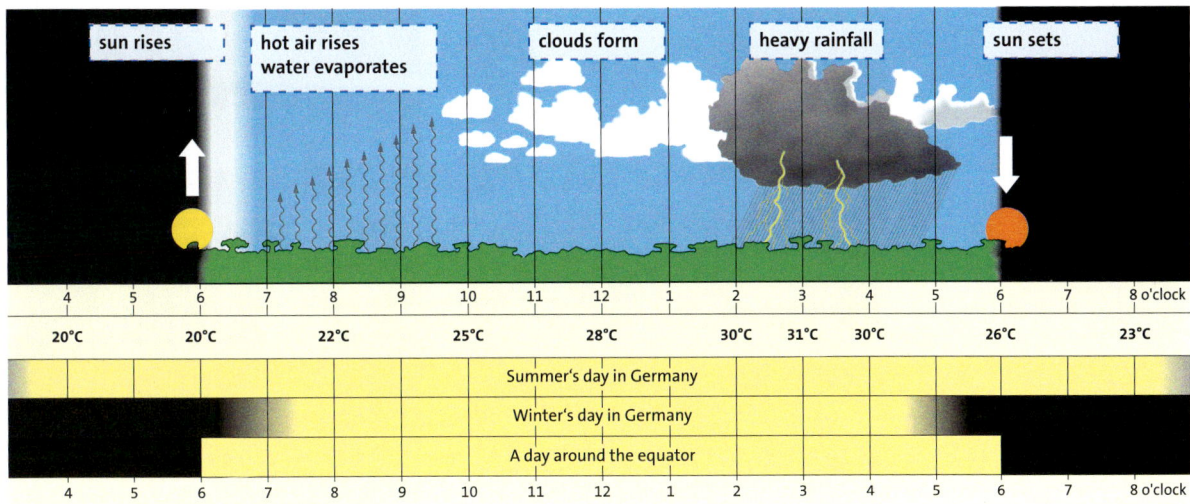

3 Aseasonal climate: a day in the tropics

"MY MAIN FEAR IS THAT WE'LL BECOME EXTINCT BEFORE WE'RE DISCOVERED."

4 Endangered species

A special climate

Rainforests are always close to the equator, correct? No, not really. They are between the Tropic of Capricorn and the Tropic of Cancer.

Figure 3 shows a day in a rainforest close to the equator. There are no seasons during the year, it is an **aseasonal climate**. There are no big temperature changes during the year but there are big changes during the day. Early in the morning, the sun rises. It gets warmer. It is very steamy in the forest. The water evaporates into the air. When the sun is at its highest point at about 12 p.m. more and more clouds form. The warmer it gets, the bigger the clouds become. Then, in the afternoon the temperatures are the highest and it starts to rain heavily. The rain cools the air and the sun sets. It gets cooler at night. There is no spring, summer, autumn and winter in **equatorial rainforests**, but there is sunshine in the morning and rainfall in the afternoon.

Other rainforests also don't have spring, summer, autumn and winter but they are not that close to the equator. There is a **rainy** and a **dry season**. These are **monsoon** and trade wind coastal climates.

to become extinct
aussterben
to discover
entdecken
Tropic of Capricorn
südlicher Wendekreis
Tropic of Cancer
nördlicher Wendekreis
aseasonal climate
das Tageszeitenklima
equatorial rainforest
äquatorialer Regenwald
monsoon
Monsun
trade wind
Passatwind
coastal
and der Küste gelegen

1 Look at the picture 1. Name the "criminal" plants which grow on this tree.
2 Use the Internet and find endangered species which live in the rainforest.
3 Interpret cartoon 4.
4 Describe the aseasonal climate in your own words (figure 3, text).
5 The rainforest is full of great animals.
a) Explain why most animals in the rainforest are active at night and in the morning.
b) Alyssa said it is very loud in the rainforest. Describe what you hear in the morning and what you hear in the afternoon.
6 Use your atlas. Make a list of the countries where you can find
– equatorial rainforests (aseasonal climate).
– tropical rainforests (monsoon and trade wind coastal climate).

7 Very wet and very hot – Tropical rainy climates

1 Waiting for rainfall

3 Flooding after monsoon rains

Rain, rain, rain

monsoon
  Monsun
precipitation
  Niederschlag
to survive
  überleben
rough seas
  unruhige See
rain gutter
  Regenrinne
coast
  Küste
vehicle
  Fahrzeug
direction
  Richtung

India has a monsoon coastal climate. But what does "**monsoon**" mean?

Some people say it's an Indian word and it means "wind that changes twice a year". In Arabic "mausim" means "wet wind" or "season".

2 Where the word monsoon comes from

From June to September you should always take an umbrella with you if you go outside. You might say this is not true, but in India it is! It is the time of the monsoon. When the monsoon period starts it rains every day. People have to follow some rules (see figure 4) which are important to survive during that time.
Every year many people don't follow these rules and die. When there is no monsoon there is only little rain. In May Mumbai only gets 11 mm of precipitation, but in July it can get up to 700 mm! This is more rain in one month than many German cities get in a whole year.

– Listen to the radio and TV to find out about strong wind or rough seas.
– Make sure that you have enough food and water with you.
– Clear and clean rain gutters.
– Stay on safe ground. Stay away from fast flowing rivers or flooded areas.
– Be prepared to leave your home if you live near a river or coast.
– Do not drive into flooded areas.
– Do what the police tells you.
– Park your cars or other vehicles on higher ground.
– Don't go fishing in small boats.

4 Safety tips during the monsoon period

Every year many pople don't follow these rules and die.

Reasons for the monsoon
To understand the monsoon, you need to know that wind always blows from H to L. and that the **ITCZ** moves. That is the reason why the monsoon changes its direction twice a year. Find out how it works:

92

Worksheet
Monsoon
104510-0703

Extra material
Climate data Mumbai
104510-0704

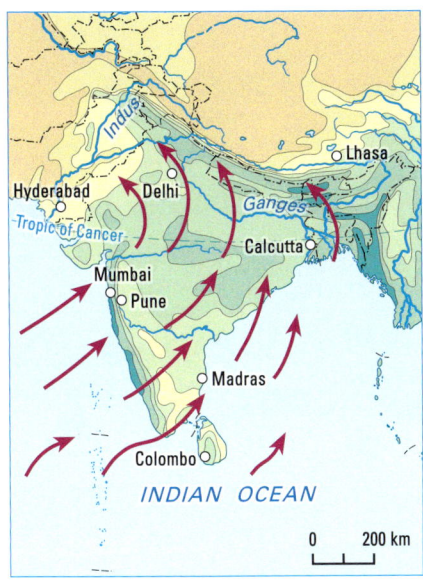

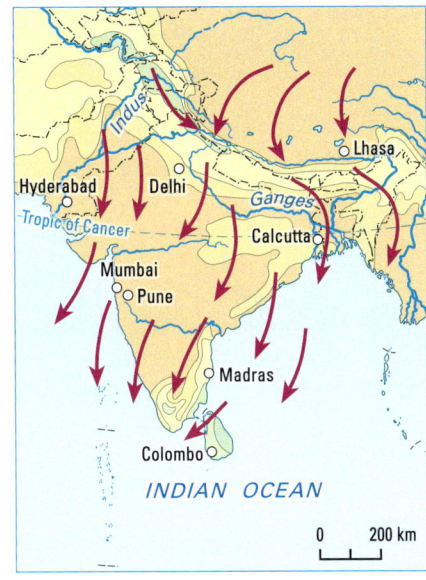

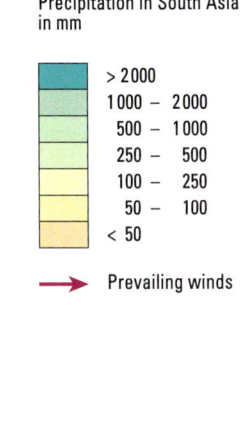
Precipitation in South Asia in mm
> 2000
1000 – 2000
500 – 1000
250 – 500
100 – 250
50 – 100
< 50

→ Prevailing winds

5 The south-west summer monsoon

6 The north-east winter monsoon

1. When there is summer in the northern hemisphere, the central parts of Asia heat up. Warm air rises and a large low pressure area (L) is near the ground. From all sides air moves in to fill up the low (L). That is why wet air masses from the Indian Ocean blow to the north (see map 5). The monsoon period starts with a lot of rainfall!

2. When there is winter in the northern hemisphere there is a high pressure area (H) over Asia because the land cools down quickly and cold air sinks down. At this time the ITCZ moves southwards towards the Tropic of Capricorn. That's why cold and dry winds blow from the cool inner continent towards the warm sea where the ITCZ is at the time (see map 6). Clear blue skies, hot temperatures and only little rainfall are typical for that time.

Monsoon – a good or a bad thing?
The heavy rainfall together with water from the Himalayas raise the water levels of the rivers. The water floods fields and its mud and silt bring many nutrients. If there's not enough rainfall in one year people won't have enough food and could die.
Regular rainfall is important for growing rice. Rice is the most important food for people in Asia.

prevailing
vorherrschend
hemisphere
Halbkugel
to heat up
erwärmen
to rise
aufsteigen
low pressure area
Tiefdruckgebiet
high pressure area
Hochdruckgebiet
mud
Schlamm
silt
Schlick

1 Explain why the rules listed in figure 4 during the monsoon period are so important.
2 List the positive and negative effects of the monsoon in a table.
3 Use the data for Mumbai (online link: 104510-0704) and draw a climate graph. Draw a second climate graph of your own city. Write a text to compare them.

4 The reasons for the monsoon are differences in pressure.
a) Say where the H and L areas are on maps 4 and 5.
b) Work with a partner: Explain the summer and winter monsoon to each other (text, maps 4 and 5).

93

Very wet and very hot – Tropical rainy climates

A young boy returns from hunting

Yanomamis making manioc

Living in harmony with nature: the Yanomami

indigenous
  eingeboren
tribe
  Stamm
border
  Grenze
plantain
  Kochbanane
manioc
  Maniok
maize
  Mais
yam
  Süßkartoffel
crop
  Feldfrucht
poison
  das Gift
to harm
  schaden

One evening Alyssa (A) finds time to talk to Nenita (N). Alyssa is fascinated by all the plants and animals in the rainforest and how people use them.

N: Hey Alyssa, how was your rainforest tour?
A: Oh, it was so great! I cannot believe how many medical plants there are in the rainforest. And how people can live in the rainforest!
N: Did you hear about the **Yanomami**? There are many indigenous tribes in the Amazon rainforest, but this tribe is special.
A: Oh really? Why?
N: Well, they live in a big area close to the border between Brazil and Venezuela. Everything they need and use comes from the rainforest. The Yanomami live in groups of up to 250 people. And all of these people live in one single house!
A: Up to 250 people live in one house? How does that work?
N: Their house, the shabono, is round and open in the middle. That's where they cook, eat, work and sit together.
A: That sounds nice, but what do they eat?
N: Well, they know how to use the rainforest without destroying it. They hunt animals, collect fruits and other things they eat, and farm around their shabono. Plantains, manioc, maize, yams, papayas and pineapples are the crops they grow.
A: Cool! These are all things we buy in the supermarket and they grow them themselves.
N: Yes, and they also know how to use the poison of frogs for hunting. The men go hunting and fishing, collect firewood and plants.
A: And the women?
N: They stay closer to the shabono. The women look after the crops, they collect fruits, cook and take care of the children. It is wonderful: they only take and use what they need. That means they don't harm the forest.

Alyssa and Nenita talk about the Yanomami

Extra material
BBC Film: Pipe Dream
104510-0705

A dense forest.

Big trees are cut down in a small area.

The trees are burnt to make an open area, the ash makes soil fertile for some years.

5 Slash and burn farming

6 A shabono

Slash and burn farming and shifting cultivation

Every three years the Yanomami move and build a new shabono somewhere else. They grow their crops in small clearings in the middle of the rainforest. How do they clear a small area of land? The Yanomami do not cut down trees. They slash and burn the area. The soil in the rainforest is not very fertile, but burning some trees and plants makes it more fertile. There are many nutrients in the ash. The ash makes it easier to grow crops. After about three years the rain washes away all the nutrients. The group has to move, and slash and burn another area. This is called **shifting cultivation**. The old clearing is left to the rainforest and natural vegetation can grow back.

Nenita told Alyssa something sad, too: "Since a few years the Yanomami have lost some of their land to people who use the rainforest and do not care if they destroy it. Not only do these people destroy the rainforest, they destroy the Yanomami's way of life, too."

slash and burn farming
  Brandrodungsfeldbau
shifting cultivation
  Wanderfeldbau
clearing
  Lichtung
soil
  Erde
fertile
  fruchtbar
nutrient
  Nährstoff
to destroy
  zerstören
pharmacy
  Apotheke

1 Look at the pictures on page 94. Describe the work and daily life of a Yanomami.

2 The rainforest is used for a lot of things.
a) Describe how the Yanomami use the rainforest.
b) Make a list of forest products you use in your daily life (internet).
c) Discuss with a partner or in a group if you really need these products.

3 Go to a pharmacy and ask about medicines made of plants which come from the rainforest. Make a list of the plants. Describe what they are used for.

Very wet and very hot – Tropical rainy climates

1 Destruction of the rainforest

destruction
  Zerstörung
to destroy
  zerstören
oygen
  Sauerstoff
poor
  arm
to settle
  siedeln
high-value
  hochwertig, hier: teuer
slash-and-burn-farming
  Brandrodung
nutrient
  Nährstoff
secondary forest
  Sekundärwald

--▶
Page 102
Exercise 2

Destroying or saving our "green lung"?

Every year about 5.8 million hectare (ha) of rainforest are cut down. Isn't that crazy? Why do we destroy the forest we need? Trees produce the oxygen we need to live!

The main reason for destruction
Because there are more and more people in poor countries they also need more land to live. So people built roads into areas where there was only rainforest before. Along these roads people settled. They cut down the high-value trees like mahogany and sold them. Then they used their area for slash and burn farming and could live there for a while. After the nutrients were gone from the soil only a secondary forest could grow. Big areas of rainforest have now been lost.

2 A bauxite mine: Bauxite is used to produce aluminium

96

 **Worksheet**
The future of the rainforest
104501-0706

 **Surf the net**
Satellite images: Destruction of rainforest in Rondonia, Brazil
104510-0707

cattle ranch
D

Who makes the money?
Companies from all over the world use the rainforest for their interests. They cut down huge areas of rainforest for cattle ranches, mining or just to get the high-value trees. When cattle ranches eat all the plants and by that all the nutrients, the soil is not fertile anymore and only a few plants can grow. Without the plants the soil is often washed away by strong rainfall. No plants mean that there is a high chance of **erosion**.
The meat of the cattle is very cheap and goes to rich countries. The poor stay hungry.
There are only four to five high-value trees per hectare. To find and transport them out of the rainforest people must build roads. With these roads large areas of the rainforest are destroyed!
Under the rainforest, people have found and have mined iron ore, gold, bauxite or oil. For this they needed to build roads again. After the mines are closed they are left in a terrible condition.

How can we save the rainforest?
In the last few years more and more organisations have started to help and act. Environmental groups like Greenpeace, WWF, FSC or Robin Wood already started to fight for the rainforest many years ago.

3 Logos

interest
 Interesse
to mine
 abbauen
erosion
 Erosion
iron ore
 Eisenerz
condition
 Zustand

1 Make a list of the dangers for the tropical rainforest. Then match the pictures at pages 96/97 with your list.
2 Write a letter to the mayor of Manaus and ask him what he does for the protection of the tropical rainforests.
3 Search the Internet for Greenpeace, WWF, ARA, Robin Wood and FSC. Make a list with their most important principles.
4 A football field has the size 0,714 ha. Calculate how many "football fields" are cut down per year, day, minute!
5 We have deforested large areas in Europe within the last 2000 years. Do we have a right to tell people in south America not to cut their trees. Discuss!

Pages 82/84
Fishbowl discussion

7 TERRA ORIENTATION

Very wet and very hot – Tropical rainy climates

In this chapter you learnt about the monsoon which affects parts of India for example. However, the monsoon winds are only a small puzzle piece in the global windsystem. There are many more windsystems around the world.

Air pressure and winds in January and July

In general differences in pressure make the air move. These differences are caused by the sun. Some parts of the world have more sunlight and are warmer than those with less sunlight. Warm air rises from the areas around, cooler air moves in to "fill this gap". Wind always blows from an area with high pressure (H) to an area with low pressure (L).

The higher the difference between H and L is the stronger the wind is.
Winds around the world never blow straight. This is because the earth rotates. That means on the northern hemisphere the winds seem to turn to the right, on the southern hemisphere to the left.
This is called **Coriolis effect (Corioliseffekt).**

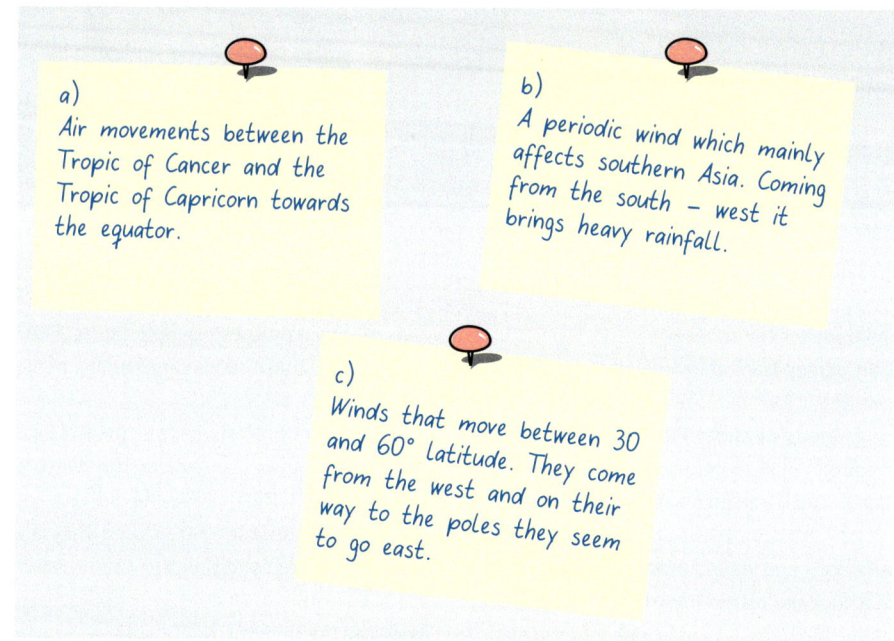

a) Air movements between the Tropic of Cancer and the Tropic of Capricorn towards the equator.

b) A periodic wind which mainly affects southern Asia. Coming from the south – west it brings heavy rainfall.

c) Winds that move between 30 and 60° latitude. They come from the west and on their way to the poles they seem to go east.

1 Definitions

– Winds blows from … to …
– towards the equator
– There is an area with low / high pressure in…

– Countries influenced by the monsoon are …

2 Phrases to help

1 Say what causes wind in about 2 sentences.
2 Look at the maps and the definitions (figure 2). Find the right definition for the following words: trade winds, monsoon, westerlies (Westwinde).
3 Work with a partner. Have a look at maps 1 and 4.

a) Tell your partner where the areas with high pressure and low pressure are around the world in January and July. One of you describes the January map, the other one the July map (maps 1 and 4, atlas).
b) Find out which countries are affected by the monsoon in January and July.

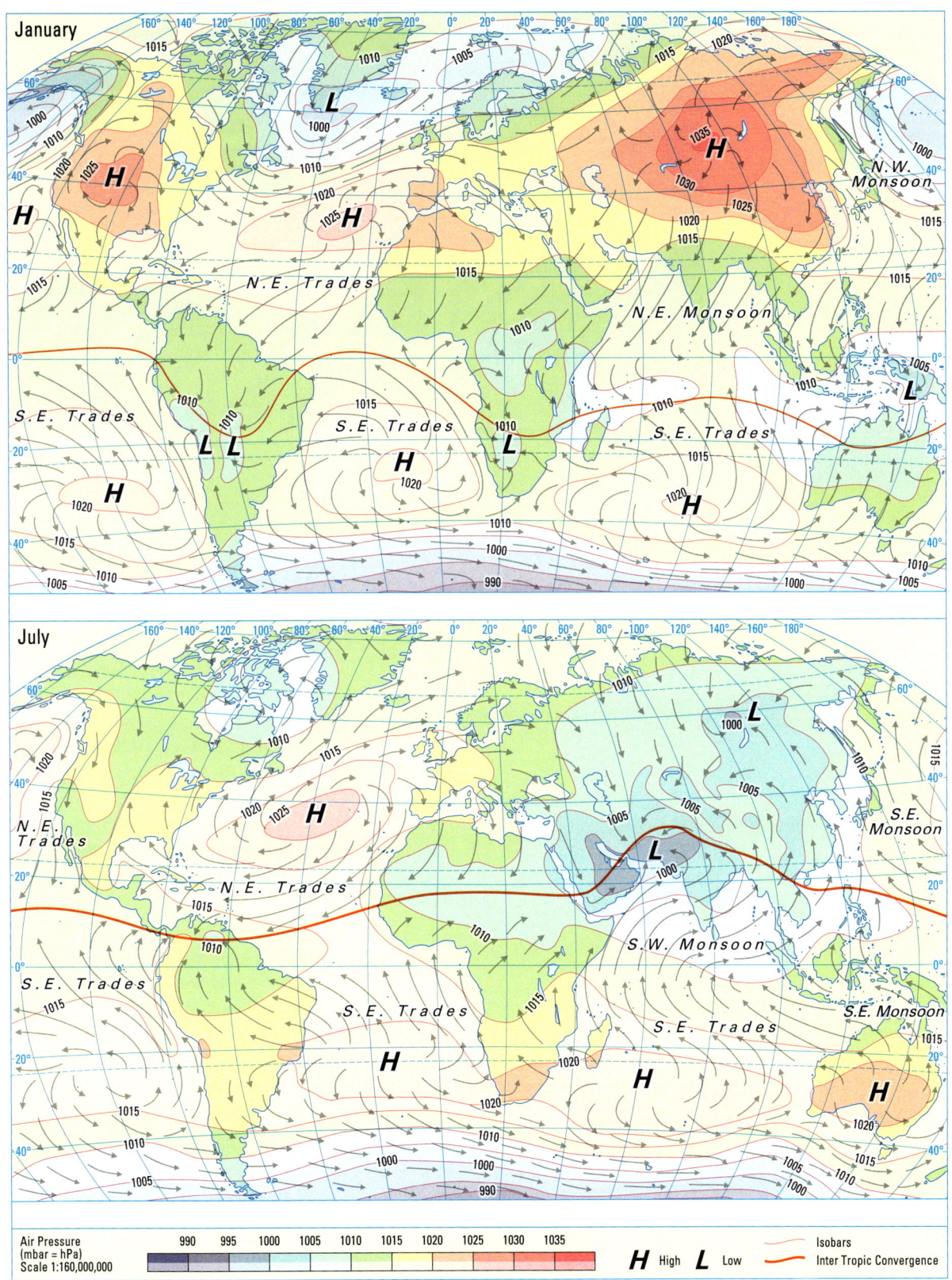

3 Air pressure and winds in January and July

99

TERRA SKILL

Thematic maps are always about certain topics. Always pay attention to the title of the map. It gives you information what the map is about.

1 Rice terraces

Working with thematic maps

Step 1: Understanding and describing the map

What is the title of the map? Is there a date given?

Which continent / country / region / city does it show?

- This map shows / is about _____
- It is from _____ (i.e. 2009).

Have a look at the key. What is shown on the map?

- The map shows _____ (continent/country/region).

Step 2: Explaining the content of the map

- The ... (e.g. blue circle) symbol stands for ... (i.e. Iron).
- The ... (i.e. dark brown) shaded areas stand for/represent ... (i.e. plantations).

What important information can you find on the map? What are the characteristics of the area?

Step 3: Evaluating the information

- There is a lot of ... (i.e. textile industry) in the north / south / west / east.
- There are ... (e.g. iron mines) in ... .
- These mines are connected by train to ... (e.g. bigger cities / the coast) where there are ... (e.g. factories / harbours).

Explain the information you found. Can you analyse the area with the help of another map? What connections can be made to other information you have? For example is there a lot of agriculture in the area (land use / agriculture map), because there is also a lot of rainfall (precipitation map)?

- The reason for _____ (e.g. a lot of agriculture) is _____ (e.g. high precipitation) .

to represent	abbilden
connection	Verbindung
pollution	Verschmutzung
destruction	Zerstörung
economy	Wirtschaft
world trade	Welthandel
energy	Energie
demography	Bevölkerungsstatistik

2 Vegetation and land use in Borneo

Thematic maps can be about:
- Nature (climate, vegetation, …),
- Environment (pollution, destruction of e.g. rainforest),
- Economy (Imports and exports, world trade, …),
- Industry (agriculture, land use, mining and energy, …),
- Demography (population growth, …).

Work with the map of Borneo.
1 State what the different colours and shades represent.
2 Analyse the map following the steps.
2 For step no. 3. Research on the Internet to find out more about land use in Borneo.

101

Very wet and very hot – Tropical rainy climates

7 TERRA TRAINING

Key words
Amazon
aseasonal climate
canopy layer
climber
humidity
emergent layer
endangered species
epiphyte
equatorial rainforests
erosion
forest floor
understorey
ground layer
indigenous tribes
monsoon
parasites
shifting cultivation
slash and burn farming
strangler
trade winds
Tropic of Cancer
Tropic of Capricorn
Yanomami

1 How the rainforest is destroyed

Focus on geography

1 Writing a letter
a) Write an email to Alyssa (see page 84). Tell her how big the Amazon rainforest is in comparison to Germany.
Explain to Alyssa why she feels tired. Tell her about the weather in Manaus.
b) Do a brainstorm: what comes from the rainforest? Tell Alyssa what could be produced in the factories she saw in Manaus.

2 People and the rainforest
Look at picture 1. Say how people destroy the rainforest (1–6).
example:
1 – slash and burn farming by big companies
2 – …

3 Right or wrong?
Correct the wrong phrases. Copy all right and corrected phrases into your exercise book.
a) It is very quiet in the rainforest.
b) It is usually very humid in the rainforest.
c) Rainforests are very dense forests because the soil is fertile.
d) The trees and plants grow tall to get more rain.
e) There are not a lot of resources in rainforests, that's why so many trees are cut down.
f) All rainforests are in aseasonal climates.

4 Odd one out
Find the words which do not go with the other words. Explain why they do not fit into the group of words.
a) South America – South East Asia – Europe – Africa
b) Banana – cocoa – orange – tea
c) Climbers – epiphytes – stranglers – emergents
d) Monsoon – aseasonal climate – dry season – trade wind
e) Equator – Tropic of Cancer – noon – Tropic of Capricorn

Focus on language
5 Word grid
There are 15 rainforest words hidden in the word grid (horizontal / diagonal).
a) Find these 15 words.
b) Explain them in your own words.
c) Give their German translation.

	a	b	c	d	e	f	g	h	i	j	k	l
1	P	A	I	N	F	O	R	E	S	T	S	O
2	R	I	E	N	D	A	N	G	E	R	E	D
3	E	T	H	U	M	I	D	E	P	E	T	I
4	C	O	I	N	S	P	E	C	I	E	S	C
5	I	F	H	D	S	O	N	O	N	C	E	T
6	P	F	O	E	L	N	S	W	R	A	N	A
7	I	E	T	R	A	D	E	W	I	N	D	T
8	T	R	B	S	S	O	S	H	V	O	U	I
9	A	S	U	T	H	W	O	Y	A	P	R	O
10	T	G	R	O	U	N	D	L	A	Y	E	R
11	I	A	N	R	O	U	T	E	L	E	B	I
12	O	E	M	E	R	G	E	N	T	A	N	C
13	N	O	W	Y	A	N	O	M	A	M	I	H

6 Alyssa stayed in a great hotel in the Amazon rainforest (pages 84 / 85)
a) Design the hotel Alyssa stayed in. Then present your ideas to your class. You want the hotel to be popular – many people should go there to see the Amazon rainforest!
b) Make a plan of the hotel resort and its surroundings. Include the buildings, the forest, the river, and so on.
c) Make a brochure or a poster about the hotel: its special location and design, sightseeing activities, etc.
d) Write a newspaper article about the hotel.
e) Make up an interview with Alyssa. Ask her about her holidays in the Amazon rainforest. You may write, film or record the interview.
f) You organise a trip to the Amazon rainforest for a class from London. Decide on what they should see and what they should learn about.

7 Picture puzzle
The three picture puzzles show words from the unit. Do you know what is meant?

a) E=A
b) 1-3
c)

8 Appendix

Here you can find important information for your bilingual geography lessons. It will help you when you want to work on your own.

Key words explained

A

Air pressure: The weight of air pressing down on the earth's surface.
Antarctica: An area south of the ➡ Antarctic Circle. Ice covers most of the continent. It is surrounded by South America, Africa and Australasia.
Antarctic Circle: 66.5°S latitude
Arctic: An area north of the ➡ Arctic Circle. It consists of the Arctic Sea, the northern parts of America, Asia and Europe.
Arctic Circle: 66.5°S latitude
Aseasonal climate: Regions between the ➡ Tropic of Cancer and the ➡ Tropic of Capricorn don't have any ➡ seasons. There are no big temperature changes during the year but there are during the day.
Atmosphere: The earth's atmosphere is a layer of gases (water vapour, ➡ carbon dioxide, ➡ methane, ozone, nitrous oxide). It protects the earth from dangerous short waves. The atmosphere consists of different layers: troposphere, stratosphere, mesosphere, thermosphere.

B

Biosphere: It is part of the ➡ geosphere. It is the home of people, plants and animals.
Black earth: It is a very fertile soil with dark brown or black colour. It often developed on ➡ loess.
Boerde: An area of very fertile land mainly in the middle of Germany. The soil consists of ➡ loess. Mainly wheat and sugar beet is cultivated there.
Boreal forest: ➡ Taiga

C

Canopy layer: One of the layers of the tropical rainforest. Trees can be up to 45 m high and form a "roof". There are a lot of different plants and animals in this layer.
Carbon dioxide: Is a ➡ greenhouse gas which can be found in the ➡ atmosphere in small amounts. The burning of fossil fuels leads to a higher amount of ➡ carbon dioxide in the atmosphere. More carbon dioxide means a higher global temperature (➡ global warming).
Coastal desert: Coastal deserts are always at the coast of landmasses. Famous examples are the Namib in Africa and the Atacama in Chile.
Condensation: Water vapour rises, gets cold and changes back from a gas into a liquid, forming clouds.
Climate: Is the average weather in a place. Weather data which was taken for about 30 years is used to describe the climate.
Climbers: Plants which have roots in the ground but use trees to climb towards the sunlight.
Cold zone: Zone in which the average annual temperature is below 0°C. Winters are long and cold.
Continental climate: A climate which can be found in regions which are far away from the sea. Hot summers, cold winters and little ➡ precipitation are typical.
Coriolis effect: The earth rotates, this has an effect on ➡ wind. On the northern ➡ hemisphere the Coriolis force shifts wind to the right and on the southern hemisphere to the left.

D

Deforestation: Cutting down forest to use the land for agriculture or settlement.
Desertification: Desertification is the spreading of deserts. Reasons are human influence but also natural causes. Most of the time it is a combination of both.
Drought: It is a dry period where a region doesn't get any or only little rainfall.
Drift ice: Pieces of floating ice on rivers, lakes or oceans.
Drip irrigation: An effective form of irrigation where water is lead through a pipe directly to the plant.
Dry savanna: ➡ savanna
Dry season: A period with little or no precipitation in the semi - humid and subtropical areas of the world.

E

Ecosystem: An ecosystem is a group of living things like plants, smaller organisms and animals in one area. They interact with non - living things like the soil, sun, earth, ➡ atmosphere or the ➡ weather.
Emergent layer: The layer with the highest of all trees in the tropical rainforest. They can be up to 60 m high.
Epiphyte: Plants which don't have roots and grow on tree trunks and branches, for example orchids.
Equatorial rainforest: The tropical rainforest can be found between the ➡ Tropic of Cancer and the ➡ Tropic of Capricorn. Trees in the forest keep their leaves all year. It is an evergreen forest. Every rainforest can have between 3 and 5 layers.

Erg: Erg is the Arabic word for sandy desert. Sand dunes are formed by ➤ wind.
Erosion: ➤ Wind and water carry the soil or the surface of rocks away.
Ethnic minority: A group of people who share the same culture (language, religion, ...), history and have special rules, living together.
Evaporation: The change of water from a liquid to a gas.

F

Furrow irrigation: A special form of ➤ irrigation where water is put on fields in large furrows. Quite a lot of water is wasted through ➤ evaporation.

G

Geosphere: The solid parts of the world and it is used together with ➤ atmosphere, ➤ hydrosphere and ➤ biosphere to describe the system earth.
Global climate model: Global climate models use a lot of numbers. They describe how the earth works. Scientists use models to find out if less sea ice or more ➤ greenhouse gases have an effect on earth. To do this they compare data from various years and can then say how our ➤ climate might change in the future.
Global warming: The way temperatures around the world are rising.
Greenhouse effect: The natural greenhouse effect keeps our earth warm by reflecting sunlight back. We put more and more ➤ greenhouse gases into the air which will make the earth even warmer. This is called the ➤ man-made greenhouse effect.

Greenhouse gas: In the ➤ atmosphere there are some gases (water vapour, ➤ carbon dioxide, ➤ methane, ozone, nitrous oxide) in small amounts. They absorb radiation from the sun. Without these our earth would be much colder. Humans put more and more ➤ greenhouse gases into the air which leads to ➤ global warming.
Ground layer: Is the lowest of the tropical rainforest layers. It consists of the forest floor and the shrub layer.

H

Hamada: It is an Arabic word and means "not fertile". One can find big stones and rocks in this desert.
Hemisphere: The ➤ equator divides the planet into a northern and southern hemisphere. The word means "half sphere".
High pressure area: An area with a higher pressure than the areas around it. In a high, air masses sink, clouds disappear and there is a high solar radiation at daytime.
Hydrosphere: One of the spheres which are part of the ➤ geosphere. Water in all forms like rivers, ice, rain or lakes makes up the hydrosphere.

I

Ice sheet: A thick mass of glacier ice on top of the land, for example in Greenland or Antarctica.
Ice shelf: Can be found for example at the edge of the Anarctic. On top it is formed by ➤ precipitation, on the bottom by sea water.

Intertropical Convergence Zone (ITCZ): An area of low pressure where the ➤ trade winds come together. The ITC follows the ➤ zenith of the sun.
Insolation weathering: The heating and cooling of rocks and minerals until they split.
Inuit: The indigenous people of the ➤ Arctic. In the past they lived from hunting and fishing.
Irrigation: Irrigation means that water is put on soil. It is usually used to make crops and plants grow in dry areas and during periods without or with only little rainfall. Two special forms of irrigation are ➤ drip irrigation and ➤ furrow irrigation.

L

Latitude: It gives the location of a place north or south of the ➤ equator. On maps one can find lines of latitude which seem horizontal. The most famous line of latiude is the equator at 0° latitude.
Lee: The side opposite from where the ➤ wind is blowing.
Lithosphere: Is the solid part of the Earth, e.g. where you stand on, where houses are built on etc.
Loess: Is a yellow material blown in by the wind from the last ice age. Today it makes the soil in the ➤ Boerde fertile.
Long wave radiation: It is also called heat radiation. It develops when ➤ short wave radiation from the sun is reflected and changed.
Low pressure area: Is a region where the pressure is lower than in the areas around it. It forms when warm air masses rise and leave low pressure at the ground.

Appendix
Key words explained

M

Man-made greenhouse effect: The man-made greenhouse effect is caused by humans. More and more greenhouse gases are put in the atmosphere and warm up the earth. The main causes are cars, a lot of cattle and industrial production.

Maritime climate: Places which are influenced by this climate are close to the sea. Typically with cool summers, mild winters and a lot of → precipitation.

Methane: Methane is a colourless → greenhouse gas which doesn't smell. It can hold more heat than → carbon dioxide.

Monsoon: A wind in south and east Asia which changes its direction twice a year. In summer it blows from sea to land, in winter from land to sea. The summer monsoon brings a lot of rainfall, the winter monsoon only little.

N

Nomads: Are people who don't settle down but move from one place to another.

North Pole: Is the most northern point of the earth's axis.

Northern hemisphere: The part of the globe north of the → equator.

O

Oasis: An area in the middle of the desert where people and animals find water. There are different kinds of oases. They get their name depending on where the water comes from, e.g. river oasis, groundwater oasis, etc.

Ozone layer: A layer in the stratosphere. It absorbs some of the dangerous → UV – waves from the sun. It makes life on earth possible.

P

Pack ice: When wind and water push → drift ice together, a huge layer of ice makes it hard for ships to go through.

Parasites: Plants which grow at the bottom of trees and use the tree's roots to get nutrients.

Permafrost: Soil which is always frozen. In summer the top layer can melt. Then there are many marshes.

Polar desert: A zone which is covered with ice and snow for most of the year. Areas which are ice free periodically have no or only little vegetation.

Precipitation: All the water coming from the → atmosphere like snow, rain or hail. Precipitation is one important part of the → water cycle.

R

Rain shadow desert: They are deserts which are "behind" high mountains (in the → lee). Wet air masses cannot cross the mountains. Therefore, areas on the other side of the mountain stay dry.

Rainy season: A period with regular → precipitation in the → tropics and subtropics.

Resource: There are different kinds of resources. They can be natural, e.g. things which come from the environment (forests, iron ore, …) or human resources (skills, things we know, …). Some resources will always be there for example water and wind power, others will come to an end (for example coal).

Raw material: Raw material are natural → resources which have not been changed or worked on. Things which can be found in nature and are used by human beings to produce something or to get energy. Examples are iron ore, wood or coal.

S

Sahel: An area between desert and dry savanna. There is only an annual → precipitation of 100 to 500 mm. It is very sensitive to droughts.

Savanna: An → ecosystem that is usually hot but with a → rainy and a → dry season. There are three types of savannas: the thorn savanna, dry savanna and wet savanna.

Season: There are four seasons (spring, summer, autumn, winter) because the axis of the earth is tilted at 23.5°. What season it is depends on whether the earth is tilted towards or away from the sun. In spring the northern → hemisphere is tilted towards the earth. In summer the sun shines directly on the northern hemisphere. Days are long and hot. More sunlight reaches the northern half of the earth. In winter the earth is tilted away from the sun. The days are shorter and colder, less sunlight reaches the northern hemisphere.

108

Semi-nomads: There is a difference to nomads because only some members of the group move from place to place. The others settle down.
Serir: A desert covered in gravel.
Shifting cultivation: A special form of agriculture in the → tropics, where → slash and burn farming is used and fields are left every few years.
Short wave radiation: The radiation send off by the sun.
Slash and burn farming: Trees are burnt, the ash makes soil fertile for some years.
South Pole: Is the most southern point of the earth's axis.
Southern hemisphere: The part of the globe south of the → equator.
Strangler: Plants which wrap themselves around the tree trunk and kill it.

T

Taiga: A vegetation zone in the northern → hemisphere. Spruce and fir are the most domintant trees there. Typical animals of the taiga are the Siberian tiger, ermine and bears.
Temperate zone: Climate zone between the → cold and subtropical zone. The climate is affected by → seasons. The average annual temperature is about 8°C.
Thorn savanna: → savanna
Trade winds: A global windsystem, air masses move towards the → equator. The → Coriolis effect makes the wind seem to go to the right in the northern hemisphere and to the left in the southern hemisphere.
Tropic of Cancer: The → latitude at 23.5 °N. On the 21st June the → zenith of the sun is there.

Tropic of Capricorn: The → latitude at 23.5 °S. The → zenith of the sun reaches the Tropic of Capricorn on 21st December.
Tropics: The part of the earth between the → Tropic of Cancer and the → Tropic of Capricorn. It is also used for the Tropic of Cancer and the Tropic of Capricorn.
Tuareg: The Tuareg are an → ethnic minority. They have travelled and traded across the desert as → nomads for thousands of years. They are also called the "blue men of the Sahara".
Tundra: An area without any trees, the soil is frozen for most of the year. Only shrubs and mosses grow.

U

Ultraviolet waves: Waves which cannot be seen by the human eye because they are so small. They are extremely dangerous to living organisms. The sun also produces ultraviolet waves but most of them never reach the surface of the earth because they are absorbed or reflected.

Y

Yanomami: The Yanomami are an → ethnic minority in the Amazon rainforest. They live in harmony with nature that means they only take things from the rainforest they really need. In the past a lot of Yanomami died because gold searchers brought diseases into their area.

W

Wadi: A valley in a desert which is usually dry all year round. When it rains they quickly fill with water.
Water cycle: The earth has a limited amount of water. The water moves around. The main parts of the cycle are → evaporation, → precipitation and outflow.
Weather: Weather is the state of the → atmosphere at any given time.
Weathering: The breaking down of rocks through temperature, → wind, pressure, air and acid. A special form is → insolation weathering.
Wet savanna: → savanna
Wind: Moving air is called wind. Wind always blows from an area with high pressure to an area with low pressure. The higher the difference between high and low the stronger the wind is.

Z

Zenith: When the sun is in the zenith its sunrays reach the earth at a 90° angle.

109

Index

All words in **bold** print are terms you can find explained in the appendix.

air pressure	12–14
Antarctica	22–25, 54
Antarctic Circle	22
Antarctic Treaty	24
anthroposphere	7
Arctic	22/23, 28/29, 49, 54
Arctic Circle	22
Aseasonal climate	91
atmosphere	6–14, 28/29, 49
barometer	15
bauxite	94/95
biosphere	6/7
black earth	44/45
Boerde	40, 44
boreal forest	32/33
canopy layer	88/89
carbon dioxide	12/13, 28, 49
cattle	75, 79, 97
coastal desert	54
climate	14, 42/43
climate graph	18/19
climbers	90
cold zone	20–39
continental climate	42
Coriolis effect	98
deforestation	81
desertification	74–77
drift ice	22
drip irrigation	46
drought	8, 47–49, 74–76, 78
dry savanna	72
dry season	16, 70–72, 75, 91
ecosystem	49, 83
emergent layer	88
epiphyte	90
equatorial rainforest	91
erg	55
erosion	44/45, 55, 77, 97
ethnic minority	58
evaporation	8, 46
fertilizer	45
flooding	48
furrow irrigation	46
geosphere	6–8
glacier	22, 48/49
global climate model	48
global warming	28/29, 48
greenhouse effect	10, 12, 28
greenhouse gas	12/13, 28/29, 49
ground layer	88/89
gravity	6, 8
hamada	55
hemisphere	16
high pressure area	93, 98/99
hydrosphere	6/7
ice sheet	22
ice shelf	22
Intertropical Convergence Zone (ITCZ)	70, 78, 92/93
Inuit	26/27, 35
iron ore	97
irrigation	8, 46/47, 76
latitude	16/17
lee	54
lithosphere	6/7
loess	44
low pressure area	93, 98/99
man–made greenhouse effect	12, 28/29
maritime climate	42
mesosphere	13
methane	28/29
monsoon	92/93
nomads	26, 58, 60, 74/75
North Pole	22
pack ice	22, 29
parasites	90
pedosphere	7
permafrost	29, 31
polar desert	54
polar region	22
precipitation	8, 14/15, 18/19
rain gauge	15
rain shadow desert	54
rainy season	16, 70–72
raw material	24
resource	63
Sahel	68–83
savanna	68–83
season	16/17
semi-nomads	58, 75
serir	55
shifting cultivation	95
slash and burn farming	95
solar radiation	12
South Pole	22
stranglers	90
stratosphere	13
taiga	32/33
temperate zone	40–45
thermometer	14/15
thermosphere	13
thorn savanna	72–74
transition zone	81
transpiration	8, 46/47
tropical rainy climates	84–103
Tropic of Cancer	16/17, 70/71, 91, 98
Tropic of Capricorn	16/17, 70, 91, 93, 98
tropics	70, 91
troposphere	13/14
Tuareg	52, 58/59
tundra	30–31
Yanomami	82, 94/95
wadi	55
water cycle	8
weather	14/15
weathering	55
weather vane	15
wet savanna	72
wind	14
wind gauge	15
zenith	16, 70, 7

Word list English – German

English	German	Example
A		
absorb	aufnehmen	Carbon dioxide **absorbs** the long wave radiation.
accumulation	Ablagerung	**accumulation** of sand
according to	entsprechend	**according to** his text
adapt	anpassen	Plants can **adapt** to the cold climate.
add	addieren, hinzufügen	to **add** some water
additional	zusätzlich	to find **additional** information
affect	beeinflussen	The area is **affected** by people.
agriculture	Landwirtschaft	A lot of water is used for **agriculture**.
aim	Ziel	The **aim** is to find an answer to the task.
air pressure	Luftdruck	The **air pressure** is less the higher you go.
allow	erlauben	It **allows** us to breathe.
amount	Menge	a huge **amount** of water
angle	Winkel	The sun shines at a right **angle**.
annual	jährlich	The **annual** average temperature of Berlin is 9.2°C.
Antarctic Circle	Polarkreis	The **Antarctic Circle** is the latitude at 66.5 north.
appendix	Anhang	In the **appendix** of this book is important information.
Arctic	Arktis	The Arctic Sea is in the **Arctic**.
Arctic Circle	Polarkreis	The **Arctic Circle** is the latitude at 66.5 south.
argon	Argon	**Argon** is an atmospheric gas.
arid	trocken	It is an **arid** region.
artificial	künstlich	an **artificial** newspaper article
aseasonal climate	Tageszeitenklima	The tropics have no seasons but an **aseasonal climate**.
atmosphere	Atmosphäre	The **atmosphere** is a thin layer of gases.
attention	Aufmerksamkeit	to get **attention**
attract	anziehen	to **attract** animals
average	durchschnittlich	The **average** temperature is … .
axis	Achse	The earth's **axis** is tilted.
B		
bark	Rinde	The tree's **bark** is very thick.
barometer	Barometer	A **barometer** measures the air pressure.
bauxite	Bauxit	a **bauxite** mine
biosphere	Biosphäre	In the **biosphere** all life is found.
black earth	Schwarzerde	**Black earth** is a very fertile soil.
boil	kochen	to **boil** water
boot	Stiefel	I wear **boots** in the tropical rainforest.
boreal forest	borealer Nadelwald	**Boreal forests** are only in the northern hemisphere.
border	Grenze	on the German **border**
boundary	Grenze	There are no **boundaries** between the spheres.
bow	Bogen	Inuit still use **bow** and arrow.
branch	Zweig	Trees have got **branches**.
breakdown	Panne	I had a car **breakdown** yesterday.

Appendix

Word list English – German

English	German	Example
breath	Atem(zug)	Let's take a deep **breath**.
breathe	atmen	**breathe** in, **breathe** out
C		
cactus pl. cacti	Kaktus, Kakteen	The **cactus** has spines. There are a lot of **cacti** in the Arizona desert.
canopy layer	Baumkronenschicht	Birds, monkeys and sloths live in the **canopy layer**.
caption	Bildunterschrift	the **caption** of the picture
carbon dioxide	Kohlenstoffdioxid	Atmospheric **carbon dioxide** absorbs heat radiation.
cattle	Rind	Too much **cattle** on a field can cause erosion.
cause	Grund	The **cause** of the monsoon is…
certain	bestimmt	In **certain** countries people don't have enough water.
clearing	Lichtung	The Yanomami grow their crops in small **clearings**.
climate	Klima	The **climate** is moderate.
climate change	Klimawandel	People often talk about **climate change**.
commercial	gewerblich	**commercial** use
conclusion	Schlussfolgerung	My **conclusion** is that…
condense	kondensieren	When air rises water vapour **condenses**.
condition	Bedingung, Zustand	They leave the mines in a terrible **condition**.
connect	verbinden	it **connects** two areas
context	Zusammenhang	It is better to use words in a **context**.
continental	kontinental	The climate is **continental** (continental climate).
continue	andauern, fortdauern	It **continues** to grow.
convince	überzeugen	You have to **convince** your classmates.
Coriolis effect	Corioliskraft/-effekt	The **Coriolis effect** seems to make winds go to the right in the northern hemisphere.
crop	Feldfrucht	They grow many different **crops** on their fields.
crop failure	Ernteausfall	When there is no rainfall, there are often **crop failures**.
D		
date	Dattel	**Dates** grow on palm trees.
decision	Entscheidung	It is your **decision**.
deforestation	Abholzung	In many countries **deforestation** is a problem.
degree	Grad	Tomorrow will be 30 **degrees**.
dense	dicht	The rainforest is a **dense**, green and tall forest.
depletion	Raubbau	**depletion** of the boreal forest
describe	beschreiben	**Describe** the picture.
desertification	Wüstenbildung	**Desertification** is a huge problem in the Sahel.
destroy	zerstören	People **destroy** the forest we need to live.
destruction	Zerstörung	the **destruction** of the boreal forest
develop	entwickeln	It has **developed** over a long time.
dig	graben	**Dig** a hole!
disappear	verschwinden	Polar bears are in danger. They might **disappear** in a few years.
disease	Krankheit	It's a terrible **disease**.

English	German	Example
disturb	stören	Don't **disturb** the birds.
diverse	unterschiedlich	The landscape is very **diverse**.
divide	(ein-)teilen	It is **divided** into four main spheres.
drift ice	Treibeis	Sometimes wind and water push **drift ice** together.
drip irrigation	Tröpchenbewässerung	**Drip irrigation** is a good way to water plants in dry areas.
domestic	einheimisch	There are **domestic** and foreign tourists in Majorca.
droplet	Tröpfchen	Clouds are made of billions of little water **droplets**.
drought	Dürre	In the Sahel there are sometimes **droughts**.
dry savanna	Trockensavanne	**Dry savannas** are one of three savanna types.
dry season	Trockenzeit	A period without or only little rain is called **dry season**.
due to	auf Grund	**Due to** the Coriolis effect...
E		
economic	wirtschaftlich	The **economic** situation is good.
economy	Wirtschaft	Niger's **economy**
ecosystem	Ökosystem	All this can effect the way **ecosystems** exist.
edge	Rand	You can find it at the **edge** of the continent.
effect	Effekt, Ergebnis	It can have dramatic **effects**.
effective	effektiv, wirksam	This method is very **effective**.
emergent layer	Schicht der Baumriesen	The **emergent layer** is the highest of all the rainforest layers.
endangered	bedroht	Some animals around the world are **endangered**.
environment	Lebenswelt	There are many different **environments**.
equatorial rainforest	äquatorialer Regenwald	**Equatorial rainforests** are around the equator.
equipment	Ausrüstung	You need a lot of **equipment** for a desert tour.
erg	Sandwüste	**Erg** is an Arabic word and means sandy desert.
erosion	Erosion	Gully erosion is a special type of **erosion**.
ethnic	ethnisch	The Yanomami are an **ethnic** minority.
evaporate	verdunsten	The sweat **evaporates** from your skin.
evaporation	Verdunstung	**Evaporation** is the change of water from a liquid into a gas.
expect	erwarten	I didn't **expect** that.
expedition	Ausflug	You can leave the ship for **expeditions**.
explain	erklären	Can you **explain** the greenhouse effect?
explorer	Forscher	A famous **explorer** was Amundsen.
extinct	aussterben	Some animals are in danger of becoming **extinct**.
F		
fear	Angst	My biggest **fear** is that...
fern	Farn	**Fern** grows in the forest.
fertile	fruchtbar	The soil is **fertile** in this area.
fertilizer	Dünger	The ash works like a **fertilizer**.
figure	Abbildung	Let's have a look at **figure** 3.
fir	Tanne	Spruce and **fir** grow there.
float	treiben	Drift ice **floats** on the surface of the ocean.
flood	fluten	Some areas are **flooded**.

Appendix

Word list English – German

English	German	Example
flooding	Überflutung	During the monsoon period there is often **flooding**.
fossil fuels	fossile Brennstoffe	Today we burn a lot of **fossil fuels.**
fresh water	Süßwasser	Some countries do not have enough **fresh water**.
fringe	Rand	The Sahel is the economic **fringe**.
frozen	gefroren	The soil in the tundra is **frozen** for most of the year.
fuel	Brennstoff	Wood is an excellent **fuel**.
fur	Fell	Animals in the tundra have thick **fur**.
furrow irrigation	Furchenbewässerung	Farmers in Spain sometimes use **furrow irrigation**.
G		
gap	Lücke	Air moves in to fill that **gap**.
glacier	Gletscher	**Glaciers** around the world are melting.
global warming	globale Erwärmung	**Global warming** is a big problem of our time.
good	Ware	Camels carry **goods** from oasis to oasis.
gravel	Kies, Schotter	A **gravel** desert has also an Arabic name: serir.
gravitation	Erdanziehungskraft	Becuase of **gravitation** air is densest at the ground.
greenhouse gas	Treibhausgas	Carbon dioxide and methane are **greenhouse gases**.
ground layer	Bodenschicht	The **ground layer** is the lowest of all rainforest layers.
groundwater	Grundwasser	Water sinks into the ground to form the **groundwater.**
gully erosion	Grabenerosion	The fields in the Boerde show **gully erosion**.
guide	Fremdenführer, (Touristen-)führer	He's a tourist **guide**. He knows about the area. You can find information in a tourist **guide.**
H		
hamada	Steinwüste	A **hamada** is the Arabic word for stony desert.
harpoon	Harpune	**Harpoons** are great for hunting.
harvest	Ernte	It was a bad **harvest** this year.
hedge	Hecke	The Mediterranean scrub is conifers, **hedges** and thorn bushes.
height above sea level	Höhe über dem Meeresspiegel	Berlin's **height above sea level** is 51 m.
hemisphere	Hemisphäre, Halbkugel	in the northern **hemisphere**
herder	Hirte	Fishermen and **herders** have different interests.
hibernate	Winterschlaf halten	In winter animals of the tundra **hibernate**.
high pressure area	Hochdruckgebiet	it is an **high pressure area**
high value	hochwertig, teuer	**high value** trees are cut down
hole	Loch	Dig a **hole**!
human	menschlich	a **human** being
humid	feucht	It is very **humid** in the rainforest.
hunter	Jäger	The Inuit are great **hunters**.
hunt	jagen	The Inuit **hunt** seals.
hydroelectric	hydroelektrisch, mit Wasserkraft	**Hydroelectric** power creates energy.
hydrosphere	Hydrosphäre	Water in rivers, lakes, glaciers, oceans, under ground and in the atmosphere makes up the **hydrosphere**.
I		

English	German	Example
ice caps	Polkappen	The polar **ice caps** are melting.
ice sheet	Inlandeis	On top of the land there are **ice sheets**.
ice shelf	Schelfeis	A special form of ice is/are the **ice shelf/shelves**.
imagine	vorstellen	**Imagine** you live in the taiga…
increase	ansteigen	The number of people visiting Majorca **increases**.
indigenous	eingeboren	They are **indigenous** people.
influence	Einfluss	It has a strong **influence** on me.
influence	beeinflussen	It can **influence** the way ecosystems work.
inhabitant	Einwohner	I live in a city with 500,000 **inhabitants**.
interact	zusammenwirken	these two things **interact** with each other
investor	Anleger, Geldgeber	The **investors** will give money to the city.
iron ore	Eisenerz	They mine **iron ore** in the rainforest.
irrigate	bewässern	Farmers need to **irrigate** their fields.
irrigation	Bewässerung	**Irrigation** is important to make plants grow.
K		
key word	Schlagwort	**Key words** are words you need to remember.
knight	Ritter	Tuareg are also called the **knights** of the desert.
L		
lack of	Mangel an	People experience a **lack of** rainfall in the area.
landscape	Landschaft	It is a beautiful **landscape**.
latitude	Breitenkreis	The equator has a **latitude** of 0°.
layer	Schicht	The atmosphere is divided into **layers**.
lazy	faul	Sloths are **lazy** animals.
lift	anheben	to **lift** up a box
limited	begrenzt	Fresh water is **limited** around the world.
liquid	Flüssigkeit	Water changes from a **liquid** to a gas when it rises.
lithosphere	Lithosphäre	The **lithosphere** is the hard and rocky outer part of the earth.
livelihood	Lebensgrundlage	Is Lake Chad a disappearing **livelihood**?
lizard	Eidechse	**Lizards** also live in the tropical rainforest.
low pressure area	Tiefdruckgebiet	The air moves to an **area** with **low pressure**.
lung	Lunge	People also call our forest "green **lung**".
M		
man-made	vom Menschen verursacht	**man-made** greenhouse effect
manioc	Maniok	Yanomami grow **manioc**.
manned	besetzt	Some research stations are permanently **manned**.
margin column	Randspalte	The vocabulary is in the margin column.
maritime	maritim	London has a **maritime** climate.
marsh	Sumpf	In summer there are many **marshes** in the taiga.
measure	messen	**measure** the temperature
mediterranean	mediterran	**Mediterranean** Sea, **mediterranean** climate
mention	erwähnen	I would like to **mention** that …
methane	Methan	**Methane** is an atmospheric gas.
melt	schmelzen	If you heat up ice it **melts**.

Appendix

Word list English – German

English	German	Example
millet	Hirse	They grow **millet.**
mine	abbauen	Iron ore is **mined.**
minority	Minderheit	Yanomami are an ethnic **minority.**
moderate	mäßig	Temperatures throughout the year are **moderate.**
molecule	Molekül	Fast moving **molecules** mean a higher temperature.
monsoon	Monsun	It rains a lot when the **monsoon** period starts.
montane	bergig	It is a **montane** desert.
mountain range	Gebirgskette	In the background of the picture is a **mountain range.**
movement	Bewegung, Transport	**movement** of air
mud	Schlamm	The river carries a lot of **mud.**
murderer	Mörder	This plant is a "**murderer**".
musk ox	Moschusochse	A **musk ox** is a typical animal of the taiga.
N		
natural greenhouse effect	natürlicher Treibhauseffekt	The **natural greenhouse effect** keeps our globe warm.
natural spring	Quelle	the **natural spring** of a river
nomad	Nomade	The Tuareg have been **nomads** for a long time.
nitrogen	Nitrat	78 % of **nitrogen** are in the atmosphere.
North Pole	Nordpol	The Arctic is the region around the **North Pole.**
nuclear weapon	Atomwaffe	No country can test **nuclear weapons** in the Antarctic.
nutrient	Nährstoff	The soil of the rainforest hasn't got many **nutrients.**
O		
oasis pl. oases	Oase	People can find water in **oases** after a long trip.
ocean	Ozean	Atlantic **Ocean**, to cross the **ocean**
opposite	gegenüber	it's on the **opposite** side
orchid	Orchidee	**Orchids** are famous house plants.
outlook	Prognose	Give an **outlook** in your presentation.
overseas	Übersee	Tourists from **overseas** often don't follow the warning signs.
overuse	übernutzen	Farmers in the Sahel sometimes **overuse** the soil.
overview	Überblick	Give an **overview** about your topic.
oxygen	Sauerstoff	Trees produce **oxygen.**
ozone layer	Ozonschicht	The **ozone layer** can be found in the stratosphere.
P		
pack ice	Packeis	The polar bear needs the **pack ice** to travel and catch seals.
parasite	Parasit, Nutznießer	**Parasites** grow their roots onto the bark of the tree.
participant	Teilnehmer	I'm a **participant** in the fishbowl discussion.
Peninsula	Halbinsel	the Antarctic **Peninsula**
permafrost	Dauerfrostboden	The **permafrost** is frozen for most of the year.
permanently	dauernd	The research station is **permanently** manned.
pharmacy	Apotheke	I'm ill I need to go to the **pharmacy.**
plantain	Kochbanane	Yanomami often use **plantains.**
poison	Gift	The Yanomami use the **poison** of frogs for hunting.
polar region	Polarregion	The areas around the North and South Pole are called **polar regions.**

English	German	Example
pollute	verschmutzen	Tourists in Antarctica **pollute** the environment.
pollution	Verschmutzung	the **pollution** of the environment
population	Bevölkerung	The **population** gets bigger.
power station	Kraftwerk	**Power stations** create electricity.
precipitation	Niederschlag	There is a lot of **precipitation** in the wet season.
protect	(be)schützen	We have to **protect** the polar bears before they will die out.
protection	Schutz	Plants are a good **protection** against wind erosion.
provide	etwas liefern	The ash of the burnt trees **provides** nutrients.
public	öffentlich, Öffentlichkeit	The **public** should know about the problems.
puzzled	verwirrt	I don't know what you mean. I'm **puzzled**.
R		
radiation	Strahlung	short wave **radiation**
rain gauge	Regenmesser	**Rain gauges** measure precipitation.
rain gutter	Regenrinne	People need to clear **rain gutters** before the monsoon starts.
rainy season	Regenzeit	Savannas have a dry and a **rainy season**.
raw material	Rohstoff	Iron ore is a **raw material**.
receive	erhalten	The plants **receive** the water directly through a pipeline.
recover	erholen	The soil needs to **recover** after people used it for many years.
recreation	Erholung	This place is for people who are looking for **recreation**.
refer	sich beziehen auf	Please **refer** to page 34 in the book!
reflect	zurückstrahlen	Short wave radiation is **reflected**.
remain	bleiben	The situation **remains** the same.
replace	ersetzen	Cooler air moves in to **replace** the warmer air.
reply	Antwort	Nenita sent a **reply** to Sean's e-mail.
represent	darstellen	The area also **represents** other regions.
research station	Forschungsstation	There are many **research stations** in Antarctica.
rise	aufsteigen	Air **rises** and cools down.
roof	Dach	Every house should have a **roof**.
root	Wurzel	Some plants have very long **roots** to reach the groundwater.
rotate	rotieren, umkreisen	The earth **rotates** around the sun.
rough	unruhig	In a storm the sea can be **rough**.
rubbish	Müll	Don't leave your **rubbish** lying around.
S		
scared	ängstlich	I'm **scared**.
scientist	Wissenschaftler	There are many **scientists** in Antarctica.
sea current	Meeresströmung	That will change the **sea currents** in the oceans.
sea level	Meeresspiegel	The **sea level** might rise.
seal	Robbe	The most important animal for the Inuit is the **seal**.
season	Jahreszeit	Germany has four **seasons**.
self-confident	selbstbewusst	Be **self-confident**.
semi	halb	They are **semi**-nomads.
sensitive	empfindlich	The Sahel is very **sensitive** towards change.
serir	Kieswüste	Gravel deserts are called **serir** in Arabic.

Appendix

Word list English – German

English	German	Example
set	untergehen	The sun **sets** at about 6pm.
settle	siedeln	Some people **settle** in oases.
severe	ernst	In some areas desertification is **severe**.
shade	beschatten	Spines **shade** the cactus and keep it cool.
shallow	oberflächlich	Some plants in the desert have **shallow** roots.
shifting cultivation	Wanderfeldbau	**Shifting cultivation** is important for the Yanomami.
short wave radiation	kurzwellige Strahlung	The sun sends off **short wave radiation**.
shortage	Knappheit	There is a huge water **shortage** in Africa.
shrub	Strauch, Busch	only **shrubs** and mosses grow
silt	Schlick	The mud and **silt** in the river bring many nutrients.
similarity	Gemeinsamkeit	England and the USA have one big **similarity**: the language.
size	Größe	The **size** of the lake has got bigger.
sky	Himmel	The **sky** is blue without any clouds.
skyscraper	Hochhaus	Big cities like Manaus have many **skyscrapers**.
slash and burn farming	Brandrodungsfeldbau	Yanomami use **slash and burn farming**.
slaughter	schlachten	Some animals need to be **slaughtered.**
sled	Schlitten	Huskies draw **sleds**.
sloth	Faultier	**Sloths** sleep for about 18 hours per day.
soil	Erde	You have to protect the **soil** from wind erosion.
solar radiation	Sonneneinstrahlung	**Solar radiation** depends on latitude.
South Pole	Südpol	The area around the **South Pole** is called Antarctica.
space	Weltraum	Some long wave radiation goes back into **space**.
species	Art	Some **species** in the rainforest are in danger.
spin	drehen	to **spin** on their own axis
spine	Stachel	Cacti have **spines**.
split	zerbrechen	Some rocks in the desert **split** apart.
spruce	Fichte	**Spruce** is a coniferous tree.
state	Zustand	it's a natural **state**
statement	Aussage, Begründung	This is an interesting **statement**.
steady	beständig	It leads to a **steady** wind in this area.
steamy	dampfig	When water evaporates the air becomes **steamy**.
stem	Stamm	Cacti store water in their **stems**.
steel pole	Stahlpfosten	Pipelines in the tundra are built on **steel poles**.
storage	Aufbewahrung, Speicher	water **storage**
strangler	Würgerpflanze	**Stranglers** are also called "murderers".
stream	(Wasser-)Strom	Two **streams** meet.
subtropical	subtropisch	Athens is in the **subtropical** zone.
sugar beet	Zuckerrübe	Farmers mainly grow **sugar beet** in the Boerde.
sunray	Sonnenstrahl	The sun sends off **sunrays**.
supply	Angebot	there is a big **supply** of bananas
suppose	annehmen, denken	I **suppose** you could be right.
surface	Oberfläche	The rays are reflected on the earth's **surface**.
surplus	Überschuss	In some regions of the world there is a water **surplus**.

English	German	Example
surround	umgeben	the **surrounding** areas
survive	überleben	It's hard to **survive** in the Sahel.
sweat	schwitzen, Schweiß	When it's warm I **sweat**. The **sweat** evaporates from the skin.
T		
temperate	gemäßigt	The climate in Germany is **temperate**.
thief	Dieb	He's a **thief**. They are **thieves**.
thorn	Dorne	Some bushes have **thorns** for protection.
tilted	geneigt	The axis of the earth is **tilted**.
trade	Handel, handeln	to **trade** with goods
trade wind	Passatwind	The **trade winds** are also called "trades".
transition zone	Übergangszone	The Sahel is a **transition zone** between savanna and deserts.
transpiration	Verdunstung	Plants use **transpiration** to let water out of their leaves.
treatment	Aufbereitung, Behandlung	waste water **treatment**
treaty	Vertrag	the Antarctic **Treaty**, to sign a **treaty**
tribe	Stamm	Yanomami **tribes** live in the middle of the rainforest.
tropics	Tropen, Wendekreise	circulation around the **tropics**
Tropic of Cancer	nördlicher Wendekreis	The sun moves up to the **Tropic of Cancer**.
Tropic of Capricorn	südlicher Wendekreis	The **Tropic of Capricorn** is the latitude at 66.5 S.
U		
understorey layer	untere Baumschicht	Smaller trees and bushes grow in the **understorey layer.**
V		
valley	Tal	An area between two mountains is called **valley**.
various	verschieden	There are **various** languages in Europe.
vegetation	Vegetation	Shrubs and mosses are the only **vegetation**.
vehicle	Fahrzeug	Inuit have motor **vehicles** to transport things.
veil	Schleier	Tuareg sometimes wear a blue **veil**.
W		
wadi	Trockental	**Wadis** quickly fill with water when it rains.
waste	verschwenden	People **waste** a lot of water.
waste water	Abwasser	**waste water** treatment
water cycle	Wasserkreislauf	The water moves around in a **water cycle**.
water vapour	Wasserdampf	That's why **water vapour** starts to condense.
weathering	Verwitterung	Insolation **weathering** is a special form of **weathering**.
well	Brunnen	**Wells** are used to get groundwater.
westerlies	Westwinde	The **westerlies** blow between 30° and 65° latitude.
wet savanna	Feuchtsavanne	In a **wet savanna** there is an annual precipitation of 1,000 – 2,000 mm.
wheat	Getreide	Farmers grow **wheat** and sugar beet.
wrap	umwickeln	The plants **wrap** themselves around the tree trunk.
Z		
zenith	Zenit, Senkrechtstand der Sonne	The sun is at its **zenith.**

Operatoren

Appendix

Anforderungsbereiche und Operatoren

Auch im bilingualen Unterricht arbeitest du mit unterschiedlichen Aufgaben. Man unterscheidet Aufgaben nach drei Anforderungsbereichen. Damit du weißt, was konkret zu tun ist, sind den Anforderungsbereichen bestimmte Verben zugeordnet, z.B. name, compare, discuss.

Anforderungsbereich I

Reproduktion

Im **Anforderungsbereich I** sollst du Sachverhalte aus einem begrenzten Gebiet so widergeben, wie du sie gelernt hast. Zusätzlich gehört die Verwendung gelernter und geübter Arbeitstechniken und Methoden dazu.

Beispiele
Name the three continents which surround Antarctica.
List positive and negative effects of the monsoon in India.
Describe how a sand dune forms in the Sahara.

Operatoren
calculate (berechnen/ermitteln): Aufgaben anhand vorgegebener Daten und Sachverhalte lösen.
describe (beschreiben): Materialaussagen und Kenntnisse mit eigenen Worten geordnet wiedergeben.
locate (lokalisieren): Einordnen von Fall-/Raumbeispielen in bekannte topographische Orientierungsraster, z.B. das Eintragen von Ländern in eine stumme Karte.
name, list (benennen, auflisten): Informationen und/oder Sachverhalte ohne eigene Wertung widergeben.

Anforderungsbereich II

Reorganisation und Transfer

Im **Anforderungsbereich II** sollst du Dinge, die du gelernt hast selbstständig bearbeiten, ordnen und erklären aber auch dein Wissen auf andere Sachverhalte übertragen.

Beispiele
Compare the climate graph of Birdsville with a climate graph of a German town.
Explain the summer and winter monsoon.

Operatoren
analyse (analysieren): komplexe Materialien oder Sachverhalte systematisch und gezielt untersuchen, auswerten und Strukturen herausarbeiten.
characterise (charakterisieren): Sachverhalte und Texte in ihren Eigenarten beschreiben und diese dann unter einem bestimmten Gesichtspunkt zusammenfassen.
compare (vergleichen): Gemeinsamkeiten und Unterschiede gewichtend einander gegenüberstellen und ein Ergebnis/eine Schlussfolgerung formulieren.
explain (erklären): Informationen und Sachverhalte (z.B. Erscheinungen, Entwicklungen) so darstellen, dass Bedingungen, Ursachen, Folgen und Gesetzmäßigkeiten verständlich werden.
interpret (auswerten): Daten oder Einzelergebnisse zu einer abschließenden Gesamtaussage zusammenführen.

Anforderungsbereich III

Reflexion und Problemlösung

Der **Anforderungsbereich III** wird von dir verlangt, dass du Probleme kritisch hinterfragst sowie selbstständig Methoden anwendest. Ziel soll sein, zu Begründungen, Deutungen, Wertungen und Beurteilungen zu gelangen.

Beispiele
Comment on the decision to close the Simpson Desert in summer.
Discuss if the following systems are open or closed systems: microwave,...

Operatoren
comment on (erläutern): Unter Abwägung unterschiedlicher Argumente zu einer begründeten Einschätzung eines Sachverhalts/einer Behauptung gelangen.
discuss (diskutieren/erörtern): einen Sachverhalt unter Abwägen verschiedener Pro- und Contra - Argumente klären und anschließend eine schlüssige Meinung entwickeln.